TERESA
of ÁVILA

TERESA of ÁVILA

Ecstasy
and Common Sense

EDITED BY
TESSA
BIELECKI

SHAMBHALA
BOSTON & LONDON
1996

Shambhala Publications, Inc.
Horticultural Hall
300 Massachusetts Avenue
Boston, MA 02115

Grateful acknowledgment is hereby given for permission to use
excerpts of previously published material from *The Collected Works
of St. Teresa of Ávila,* volumes 1, 2, and 3, translated by Kieran
Kavanaugh and Otilio Rodriguez © 1976 by the Washington
Province of Discalced Carmelites, ICS Publications, 2131 Lincoln Rd.
NE, Washington, DC 20002, USA; and from *The Letters of Saint
Teresa of Jesus,* volumes 1 and 2, translated by Professor E. Allison
Peers, reprinted by permission of Burns & Oates, Ltd.

Distributed in the United States by Random House, Inc., and in
Canada by Random House of Canada Ltd

Library of Congress Cataloging-in-Publication Data

Teresa, of Avila, Saint, 1515–1582.
[Selections. English. 1996]
Ecstasy and common sense / Teresa of Avila; edited by Tessa
Bielecki.
p. cm.
ISBN 1-57062-167-5
1. Spiritual life—Catholic chuch. 2. Meditations.
3. Mysticism. I. Bielecki, Tessa. II. Title.
BX2179.T3E5 1996   96-13513
248.2'2—dc20   CIP

BVG 01

For my friends
Jorge, Juan, Lucho, and Concha,
who speak in Teresa's voice
and help me see her in the flesh;
and for Laurance, who made this book possible.

CONTENTS

ACKNOWLEDGMENTS

TERESA of Ávila: my namesake, my patron saint, my best woman friend; I feel closer to her than any earthly woman. This warrior-bride and I spend a lot of time together, since this is my third book about her in three years. We laugh together, we weep, we share the anguish and the joy of creating new contemplative communities to provide our broken world with hope, vitality, and sanity. I see Teresa's face; I hear her voice. As my new friend Paul wrote: "You hold the pen, and Teresa holds you."

I wrote the first book at Nada Hermitage in the desert of southern Colorado, when my community generously freed me of my leadership responsibilities for several months and gave me a kind of sabbatical. I wrote the second at Nova Nada, deep in the woods of Nova Scotia, when I was thoroughly immersed in those responsibilities again. I completed this volume in the midst of founding our third center, Holy Hill, in the lush green fields of Skreen, County Sligo, Ireland. It was the most difficult time of my life, devoid of ecstasy. The commonsense business of meeting a publishing deadline helped keep me grounded. I am grateful to Shambhala for the challenge of presenting Teresa to a brand new readership.

I am also grateful to the Institute of Carmelite Studies

and to Burns and Oates who have given us their superb twentieth-century translations of Teresa's writings. This is the third time they have permitted me to quote extensively from their work. Please help me thank them by turning from these selected passages to the original Teresian sources.

Nothing I ever do would be possible without the love and support of my incredible community. The research they helped with three years ago is the essence of this book. Cecilia McGowan was my computer expert, translating my scribbled handwritten pages into manuscript form. She is also the one who coined the crucial phrase "spirituality for the long haul." Father Tom Renaud's epic poem on the life of Teresa is the basis of my introduction. And I would have been lost at Holy Hill without Susan Ryan and her typing, singing, and soul-friending.

Most of all, I must thank the community for the life we've shared these past thirty years. Through the wonder, bravado, disillusionment, and shattering we've suffered together in first naive and then well-seasoned innocence, I have come to understand the five stages of spiritual growth. Now I rejoice with these faithful companions and friends as we move steadfastly together into deeper glory.

—Mother Tessa Bielecki
Easter 1996

SOURCE ABBREVIATIONS

CO   *Constitutions*

F   *Foundations*

IC   *The Interior Castle*

LE   *Letters*

L   *Life*

P   *Poetry*

SC   *A Satirical Critique*

S   *Soliloquies*

SS   *Meditations on the Song of Songs*

T   *Spiritual Testimonies*

VI   *On Making a Visitation*

W   *The Way of Perfection*

Excerpts from letters are from *The Letters of Saint Teresa of Jesus*, volumes 1 and 2 (London: Burns & Oates); All other excerpts are from *The Collected Works of St. Teresa of Ávila* (Washington, D.C.: ICS Publications, 1976).

THE WOMAN
and the
WISDOM

*Teresa's passionate, ideal nature
demanded an epic life.*

—GEORGE ELIOT, *Middlemarch*

S AINT TERESA was born with a warrior's heart locked inside a woman's body. This produced a tension in her so crucifying and yet so creative it tore her apart, then restored her to wholeness on the highest levels of human integration and intimacy with the Divine.

Teresa was born in 1515 in Ávila, Spain, noble city of saints and songs, where the summer sun is scorching and winter winds from the surrounding mountains chill the bones. Ávila today looks much as it did in Teresa's time, an enclosed fortress of stately turrets and spires, once defended from an attacking enemy by the women of the city, led by the legendary Jimena Blasquez, while their knights were far from home.

The high arts of chivalry pervaded Ávila in its prime.

Young Teresa, a bright and lively child, yearned for an epic life of her own. Tales of quests for the Holy Grail set her afire. She shared these tales with her frail and lonely mother in a conspiracy against her pious father, who preferred his wife and daughter to read the more sobering lives of the saints.

Teresa dreamed of doing knightly deeds. She acted out chivalrous quests in the courtyard with her brothers and cousins. She built stone huts in the garden and played hermit. At the tender age of seven, she persuaded her favorite brother, Rodrigo, to set out on foot with her to seek a bloody martyrdom at the hands of the Moors, recently driven out of Spain into North Africa by King Ferdinand and Queen Isabella. Her desire was thwarted by an uncle who discovered the children outside the walls as he was returning to the city. The place is marked today by a charming monument that affords a dramatic view of Ávila rising from the rolling Castilian plains.

Much later and much wiser, at the age of twenty, Teresa ventured out a second time, leaving the ease of her father's house to enter the Carmelite Convent of the Incarnation. The newly widowed and lonely Don Alonzo had wanted to keep his favorite child by his side, but Teresa conspired against him again; she escaped from the house and entered the convent in secret. This broke not only her father's heart, but her own as well: "It seemed that every bone in my body was being sundered." (Don Alonzo later approved and sent a good dowry.)

Teresa threw herself into the monastic rhythms at the

convent with characteristic passion. She loved the life but found it difficult. Before she entered the convent, a romantic attachment to one of her cousins had led her to contemplate marriage, yet she feared it because marriage enslaved women in her day.

Always an extremist, Teresa strove with a brittle valor to live a flawless life. Impatiently she subdued her will with a harsh, misguided pride. Under the strain, so antithetical to her exuberant nature, she became gravely ill and eventually paralyzed. Shattered in spirit as well as body, she lay in bed for three long, painful years that purified her intention. When finally she was able to leave her bed and crawl on hands and knees, she wept with grateful tears and blessed St. Joseph for her healing.

Yet Teresa's pride sprang up in new form and grew to do more harm. She was seduced by the convent parlor, where the nuns entertained family, friends, and benefactors. Miraculously cured, more witty and charming than ever, Teresa became the center of attention. She filled her days with empty talk. Many an hour was wasted until many a year was lost. She neglected her solitary prayer and then gave it up altogether. Years later, she wrote scathing paragraphs condemning such lukewarmness and mediocrity.

As Teresa tells the story, one day Christ rescued her from her deadly, trivial airs, from weak, halfhearted virtues and cold, halfhearted prayers. Rounding the corner of a hallway, she came upon a statue of Jesus scourged at the pillar en route to His crucifixion. The sight of such innocent suffering and profound love awakened a river of tears and filled the repentant woman with new fervor.

Teresa never strayed from her beloved Christ again. Deep in her heart, she began to nurture a silent revolution. The parlor was not the only distraction; there were more serious impediments to growth at the convent. Teresa dreamed of a more austere way of life that would lead to deeper mysticism and greater vitality.

Almost thirty years after entering the convent, Teresa left in 1562 with a handful of brave companions to found a new, reformed monastery, which she named after St. Joseph. It was small and simple, in a tiny corner of Ávila, farther away from the protection of the city walls and seemingly no threat to anyone.

Yet Teresa's Carmel created an enormous uproar. All the strength of Ávila, the best of that chivalrous town, tried to tear down the doors, discredit Teresa, and destroy her fledgling reform. But the power of Ávila could not prevail against the strength of her powerlessness. The gates of her first foundation hold to this very day. The story of what happened after St. Joseph's is even more exciting.

Why is this sixteenth-century Spanish mystic a model for contemporary men and women? Teresa dared to make an impossible dream come true. The story of her "holy daring" is not only entertaining reading, it gives us inspiration to dream our own dreams and courage to follow them. (I have developed this extensively in *Teresa of Ávila: Mystical Writings*.)

Teresa spent five relatively quiet years at St. Joseph's and intended to die there in obscurity. Then she was thrust out into a life so public and so bold, even the king of Steve knew her name. Sharp as a sword of Toledo, bright as a sun-drenched plain, firm as the stone towers of Ávila, Teresa harnessed not only her mules but the deep recesses of her warrior energy. Then she traveled the Spanish countryside, using her parlor charm and wit for a mighty purpose.

She charmed noble knights and pompous bishops, greedy merchants and petty bureaucrats, charmed them all for the sake of her Lord, for the sake of her pillared Christ. She walked His royal road, bearing a seed of fire that ignited not only Spain but the rest of Europe and eventually the world.

Teresa set out from St. Joseph's in 1567 and founded sixteen more monasteries, which still exist. With the help of Saint John of the Cross and other conquistadors of the spiritual life, she also founded monasteries for men and served as their spiritual mother. The lyrical poetry of John of the Cross is considered among the best in world literature; it was composed while he was imprisoned for his role in Teresa's reform.

Hands that had known a soft and gentle life grew rough and cracked from the arduous work in Teresa's houses—and more beautiful to the High King of Heaven. Teresa's followers learned that love leads to costly sacrifice. The years were far from easy in these rugged Carmels, but they rang with laughter and shone with a lordly fire. In joy and pain, they produced a fertile spiritual legacy that enriches us today.

Through years of travel and trials, through enemies without and even within the Church and the Carmelite Order, through health that steadily worsened, Teresa's courage did not waver. Her warrior's heart was ever "manly" and "determined to fight." She poured out all her energy and spent all her blood, her passionate love for Christ her King shining wherever she went.

Her rigorous outer life was matched by an equally intense inner life. Teresa labored and struggled, argued and negotiated. She wrote interminable letters and wove her way through delicate business deals and intricate lawsuits. She robbed herself of sleep in order to pray and write her mystical treatises.

And all the while, "His Majesty" led her deeper into the sacred chambers where He hid His greatest treasure. Christ the Bridegroom led His bride into the palace of glory, where an arrow of fire pierced her heart in a blaze of blood and wine. The magnificent sculpture by Gian Lorenzo Bernini, now housed in the Church of Santa Maria della Vittoria in Rome, depicts the almost orgasmic ecstasy of this experience, known as the "transverberation."

In this mysterious realm of being, which Teresa later called the Interior Castle, her desire found completion. Here the Divine Bridegroom gave her His love a hundredfold for every tear she shed. "No wonder we have to pay what seems to us a high price," Teresa wrote. "The time will come when you will understand how trifling everything is next to so precious a reward."

But Teresa never had the luxury of lingering long in this love chamber, in this inner wine-cellar of divine intoxication. God sent her out again and again to carry His brave banner (the "heraldry" of His five wounds) and manifest His love in an anguished and loveless world.

Teresa worked full-tilt till she was sixty-seven. Then, ill and weak, and far from her beloved Ávila where she desperately needed to rest, she was ordered to make an arduous journey for the absurd purpose of consoling a benefactor's daughter-in-law in childbirth. (Ironically, the child had already been born.)

The journey was disastrous for Teresa. Her warrior's heart began to fail, and her pulse grew dim. She who had burned so long with the light of Christ, at last burned out for Him. She died on October 4, 1582, repeating over and over, "I am a daughter of the Church." Because the new Gregorian calendar was introduced that year, the day following Teresa's death became October 15, which is still celebrated as her feast day. Already acclaimed a saint by the people in her own lifetime (to her utter horror), Teresa was officially canonized in 1622, forty years after her death. Paul VI declared her the first woman Doctor of the Church in 1970.

Today hundreds of Teresa's Carmelite monasteries span the globe. From her initial seed of fire grew a blazing spirituality that still ignites the hearts of ordinary men and women everywhere who strive to embody the universal Teresian spirit and grow into the heights of mystical marriage with the Divine Bridegroom.

TERESA
of ÁVILA

SPIRITUALITY
for the
LONG HAUL

*Blessed be the trials that even here
in this life are so superabundantly
repaid.* (L 11.5)

THROUGHOUT two thousand pages of her writings, Teresa gives us concrete and practical advice for spiritual growth. Using more contemporary language, we can translate the various stages she describes along the spiritual path as Wonder, Bravado, Disillusionment, Shattering, and Glory. Along this way, we encounter obstacles and roadblocks; we make mistakes and fall repeatedly into ruts. But if we are determined to persevere "come what may, happen what may, whatever work is involved, whatever criticism arises . . . or if the whole world collapses," we enter into that highest stage of growth and glory, intimacy with the Divine.

THE WEB OF WONDER

We wake up in a web of wonder with a deep sense of mystery. Looking to the wisdom of the Jewish tradition, we see ourselves like Adam and Eve waking up in the Garden of Eden, brand new, innocent, and green.

Saint Teresa was full of wonder over all of creation: coconuts and cold melon, fresh eggs and quinces, colored fountains and orange-flower water, perfume and poetry, music and dancing, books and reading, fields and flowers, gardens and good soil, earth, air, fire, and especially water. She even described the stages of growth in prayer in terms of watering a garden. She loved nature and recommended that we turn to it when we have trouble praying: "Go someplace where you can see the sky and walk up and down a little."

She was so fond of sardines that she said she could be bribed with one. The story is told of Teresa's sisters discovering her in the kitchen, enthusiastically devouring a partridge. Responding to their shocked protestations, Teresa exclaimed: "When I fast, I fast; and when I eat partridge, I eat partridge!"

Teresa was full of wonder over the beauty of human friendship, and even more over human friendship with the Divine through the wonder of prayer. For Teresa, prayer was not the rote and mechanical recitation of ready-made prayers but an "intimate sharing between friends." As she wrote in her *Life:* "God and the soul understand each other. . . . It's like the experience of two persons here on earth who love each other deeply and understand each other well."

This intimacy with the Lord of Creation takes place deep within the Interior Castle. "Within us lies something incomparably more precious than what we see outside ourselves," Teresa marveled. "Let's not imagine we are hollow inside."

THE ROYAL ROAD

Once we awaken to the wonder of the inner life, we set out on the spiritual path Teresa calls the "royal road." We must make a noble effort to begin well and then persevere "like soldiers," full of "determination to die rather than fail to reach the end of the journey." We need to cultivate lofty thoughts and are greatly helped by spiritual guidance, good reading, and the regular practice of prayer. For Teresa, prayer is a rugged and robust exercise. "May God deliver us from foolish devotions," she cries. She recommends a simple and highly personal method: Look at Christ who is looking at you.

HARD WORK AND VIRTUE

The royal road requires hard work and virtue: concern for others expressed in deed and not mere talk, ego annihilation through a hardy obedience and detachment from self-satisfaction, trust and humility "in the presence of infinite Wisdom." We must have a good sense of humor and laugh at ourselves. We must also have a healthy dose of common sense.

Teresa is practical, sensible, and down to earth. "God deliver me from people so spiritual they want to turn everything into perfect contemplation," she exclaims. She focuses on both the spiritual *and* temporal aspects of life, on "good order," "harmonious organization," "rule and measure." Virtue is more important to her than austerity. She emphasizes the need for good food, ample sleep (no less than six hours), and the value of recreation as well as discretion.

B R A V A D O   A N D   B E Y O N D

The bravado phase along the spiritual path is one of naive enthusiasm. We experience our own strength, energy, and vitality—which leads to excessive self-reliance and overconfidence. We think we can do anything. This stage is inevitable and often necessary to get us going along the royal road.

But there are many dangers here: false security, presumption, a carelessness and complacency that lead us to neglect small matters that all too soon become larger ones. Still enslaved by "a thousand vanities," we suffer from fragmentation, a "tempestuous" interior battle: "What hope can we have of finding rest outside of ourselves if we cannot be at rest within?"

Our talk here is still cheap. We don't need more polite words but heroic deeds. We need to move beyond mere bravado. But we are so bogged down in the mud at this stage, we suffer relapses, fall flat on our face, and return to past faults we thought we had overcome.

Because Teresa experienced so many downfalls in her own life, she consoles and encourages us: "Don't become discouraged and stop striving to advance. For even from this fall God will draw out good, as does the seller of an antidote who drinks some poison to test whether his antidote is effective."

In her astute wisdom, Teresa teaches us how to move beyond bravado through healthy self-knowledge and self-doubt, vigilance, perseverance, and courage. We must be like "strong men," "manly" and "determined to fight"—in other words, spiritual warriors, engaged in spiritual warfare. Teresa worries about those who seem to be too quiet and always at peace because "to be without war is impossible." We must fix our eyes on Christ, for all our trouble comes from not keeping our focus on Him.

MISTAKES, RUTS, AND ROADBLOCKS

As we struggle to keep moving and growing, we encounter innumerable roadblocks and make more mistakes. We are still selfish and self-indulgent, fussing about our health, our need for rest, for tranquillity and order. "The body grows fat and the soul weakens," laments Teresa.

We are distracted by our desire for money, prestige, and human approval when there is no danger so obvious "as this concern about honor and whether we have been offended." We disperse our energy through inane conversation (a "noxious form of recreation"), overinvolvement in superficial worldly affairs, and compulsive, unnecessary business and overwork. Even our own families can obstruct us along the path. Predating John Bradshaw and other "family systems" psychologists, Teresa warns against "the harm that is caused from dealing with relatives."

We finally make the biggest mistake of all. After sporadically neglecting our prayer, we abandon it altogether. Teresa is emphatic about our blindness here: we court danger and go from bad to worse. Then this "folly" puts us "right in hell"—not after we die, but here on earth.

DISILLUSIONMENT

Eventually, every vestige of bravado fades away. The honeymoon is over. Disillusionment sets in on every level of life: personal, social, spiritual; marriage, family, business, profession. Teresa is really articulate about her experience at this stage: "There come days in which one word alone distresses me, and I would want to leave the world because it seems everything is a bother to me."

As she wakes up beyond bravado in the wonder of her own weakness, she calls herself "gloomy" and "illtempered" and admits that she often gets so angry she wants to "eat everyone up, without being able to help it." As her disillusionment grows, she describes herself as a helpless little bird with broken wings or a stupid little donkey grazing.

When we reach this stage, we become discouraged, because we no longer understand ourselves and our real motivation. We are weak and cowardly on the moral level and see that "our natural bent is toward the worst rather than the best." We find ourselves so physically limited and unfree that we are even affected by "changes in the weather and the rotating of the bodily humors." We are resistant to and even repulsed by what should attract us. Teresa came to hate the hour of prayer so much that all she could do was listen for the clock to strike the end of the hour.

All around us and in ourselves we see mendacity: deception, duplicity, and lies. As Teresa notes, the world is a mockery, a joke, "as good as a play." We are stunned by our experience of impermanence, instability, and insecurity. We try to protect ourselves because we are afraid of the truth that haunts our sleeping and sometimes even our waking hours, the truth that the Buddhist and Hindu traditions call *samsara:* Everything changes, passes, and dies—and so will we. As Teresa wrote in her famous bookmark prayer: "Todo se pasa"—all things are passing.

Returning to the imagery used in the Jewish tradition, we are no longer like Adam and Eve in the Garden of Eden, we are exiled from Eden. We feel this keenly in our prayer, which seems vapid, distasteful, and dry. We are distracted and can't concentrate. The mind wanders and clatters on like a grinding mill, a frantic madman, or "little moths at night, bothersome and annoying."

We need to move into the realm of silent prayer because God is "near." Teresa tells us, "It isn't necessary to shout in order to speak to Him." He understands us "as if through sign language." We must learn to pray "not with the noise of words but with longing."

This is a crucial transition in our lives. Most of us make a fatal mistake here. We try to run and hide, close our eyes, mask the pain. We commute back to bravado. We go backward instead of forward. Why? Because we have a vague sense of what lies ahead, and it paralyzes us.

SHATTERING

In this stage, our hearts finally break. We enter a terrible crucible where everything we hold dear is shattered: projects and plans, hopes and dreams, little loves and big loves. We have gone beyond mere disillusionment. At this stage, all our illusions are *shattered.*

This comes about in many ways: the loss of a loved one through death, disease, absence, or separation, even the dying of love; the loss of a beloved animal, object, or place; the loss of a cherished job or promotion. We can be shattered by the experience of our own illness, aging, and death; or the even more painful experience of our own psychological woundedness or our moral or mental weakness.

Our interior suffering is so dreadful it "breaks and grinds the soul into pieces." We are assailed by "a thousand doubts and suspicions" and don't know what to do with ourselves. Our fear is so intense, we feel as though we are drowning or going insane. We suffer misunderstanding, criticism, opposition, and the betrayal of friends who take "painful bites" at us. We are so tormented that we can't pray and don't understand what we read. We can't stand to be with others, but we hate to be alone. Then we end up hating ourselves.

Our anxiety over others is an acute affliction. Teresa worried when her friends ate bad fish, preached too many sermons, neglected to take their medicine, fell off their mules, or drank sarsaparilla water. She agonized over the persecution of her renewal and the imprisonment of John of the Cross, calling it a "piteous story." It hurt her more to see her loved ones suffer than to suffer herself.

But suffer she did. She was shattered by illness, loneliness, overwork and worry, exhaustion, and "the grip of depression." "So many troubles are descending on me all at once," she wrote. "You would be shocked if you knew about all the trouble I am having here, and all the business I have to do—it is killing me."

The Christian tradition is strong in its wisdom about this stage of human life. We call this "crucifixion." We understand that our Garden of Paradise is a *crucified* paradise. Our Garden is not only Eden, but Gethsemane and Golgotha: the place of the skull and the cross.

For the Christian, the cross is not a negative symbol of death, despite the very real horror of crucifixion. It is a symbol of life and resurrection. Teresa wrote three poems describing the cross in ecstatic, positive, life-giving terms, calling it the "Tree of Life." If we are faithful to the cross and the painful process of shattering it brings, we move into the fifth and final phase.

GLORY

The scriptural term for this phase is glory. Once again we find ourselves like Adam and Eve, only better: re-awakened and brand new, with an innocence both child-like and seasoned, filled with wonder on the *other* side of pain.

We do not have to wait till we die to enjoy this glory. We begin to know it "even from here below." We reach a point of such victory, we sprout wings and fly! We are ready to risk all for God because we know that in losing all we gain all.

In a spirit of freedom, peace, surrender, and holy indifference, we "accept the bitter as happily as we do the delightful." We "forget about pleasing ourselves in order to please the one we love." We say with Teresa, "I no longer need rest but the cross." In our "exalted" state, we are more humble than ever, for we know by experience that without humility, "everything goes wrong."

Our prayer now is no longer work but glory: "One moment is enough to repay all the trials that can be suffered in this life!" We also understand clearly that our contemplation is not for our own enjoyment but to give us the "strength to serve." Teresa describes the paradox: "Love turns work into rest."

DIVINE INTIMACY

We are "chastised with glory" and come out of the crucible of suffering "like gold, more refined and purified." Shattering erases our boundaries, removes our limitations, and makes us ready for the greatest glory of all. "May You be blessed forever and ever, my God," prayed Teresa, "for within a moment You undo a soul and remake it." Teresa is clear: she would not exchange all her suffering for all the world's treasures. "Oh, oh, how well He pays! And He pays without measure!"

How does He "pay"? With divine intimacy, bridal mysticism, spiritual marriage: "God espouses souls spiritually," and "two fires become one." This blessing is the "greatest that can be tasted in this life." At this stage prayer is loving, for "progress does not lie in thinking much but in loving much."

For those with a temperament like Teresa's, divine intimacy is often accompanied by ecstasy, holy intoxication, and wounds of love. Teresa calls it a "heavenly madness," "glorious foolishness," and a "delightful disquiet." She admits that this "seems like gibberish" and "doesn't make sense," so she is forced to "speak in absurdities." Her joy is so unbearable, she "speaks folly in a thousand holy ways." Using the passionate and erotic language of the bride in the *Song of Songs,* she cries out: "Kiss me with the kiss of your mouth," "My God and my Glory, Your breasts are better than wine." Then she concludes, "May we all be mad for love of Him who for love of us was called mad."

This madness is reflected most strongly in our love for the cross, which we experience even at this highest level of spiritual development. "Whether in the beginning, the middle, or the end," proclaims Teresa, "all bear their crosses, even though these crosses be different." In no uncertain terms she describes the great joy we may find in suffering at this stage: "What a tremendous good it is to suffer trials and persecutions for Him. For the increase of the love of God I saw in my soul and many other things reached such a point that I was amazed."

Teresa freely chose suffering as a way of being more intimately united with her beloved Spouse—"if there were no other gain." But remarkably enough, "there are always so many other benefits"—rest, protection, strength, consolation, and life itself. This is Teresa's strongest conviction, greatest madness, and deepest intimacy. She urges the rest of us to walk along this same path.

There is a chronic tendency in all of us to seek out easy spiritualities that promise immediate and self-gratifying results after very little effort. These short-term "feel-good" pseudospiritualities fall apart at the first challenging moments of disillusionment and cannot withstand the process of shattering that eventually ravages us all. Teresa's spirituality, on the other hand, steeped in the Christian Mystery of Crucifixion-Resurrection (the "Paschal" or "Passover" Mystery), offers us a spirituality for the long haul.

Teresa continues to inspire us even four hundred years after her death. Her teaching has the power to see us through a lifetime and will endure hundreds of years after us, because the wisdom is perennial.

Where do you find yourself today? Whether you are delighted or disillusioned, filled with wonder or wounded, shining or shattered, Teresa has a word of wisdom just for you.

2

THE WEB
of
WONDER

LORD OF CREATION

Lord, You are on the earth and clothed with it. (W 27.3)

O my God, God, God, author of all creation! And what is creation if You, Lord, should desire to create more? You are almighty; Your works are incomprehensible. (S 8.1)

It helped me to look at fields, or water, or flowers. In these things I found a remembrance of the Creator. I mean that they awakened and recollected me and served as a book and reminded me of my ingratitude and sins. (L 9.5)

I don't find anything more appropriate to explain some spiritual experiences than water; and this is because I know little and have no helpful cleverness of mind and am so fond of this element that I observed it more attentively than other things. In all the things that so great and wise a God has created, there must be many beneficial secrets, and those who understand them do benefit, although I believe that in each little thing created by

God there is more than what is understood, even if it is a little ant. (IC IV.2.2)

No wonder the saints, with the help of God, were able to do with the elements whatever they wanted. Fire and water obeyed St. Martin; even the birds and the fish, St. Francis; and so it was with many other saints. (W 19.4)

What would happen if we knew the property of every created thing? It is very beneficial for us to busy ourselves thinking of these grandeurs. (IC V.2.2)

O my Jesus! Who could make known the majesty with which you reveal Yourself! And, Lord of all the world and of the heavens, of a thousand other worlds and of numberless worlds, and of the heavens that You might create. (L 28.8)

The sisters were delighted to see the coconuts, and so was I. Blessed be He Who created them: they are certainly something worth seeing. (LE 185)

MATTER MATTERS

God deliver me from people so spiritual they want to turn everything into perfect contemplation no matter what. (SC 7)

The Lord walks among the pots and pans. (F 5.8)

We are not angels, but we have a body. To desire to be angels while we are on earth—and as much on earth as I was—is foolishness. Ordinarily, thought needs to have some support. If at times the soul goes out of itself or

goes about so full of God that it has no need of any
created thing to become recollected, this isn't so usual.
(L 22.10)

To be always withdrawn from corporeal things and enkindled in love is the trait of angelic spirits, not of those
who live in mortal bodies. It's necessary that we speak
to, think about, and become companions of those who,
having had a mortal body, accomplished such great feats
for God. How much more is it necessary not to withdraw through one's own efforts from all our good and
help, which is the most sacred humanity of our Lord
Jesus Christ. (IC VI. 7.6)

When one is in the midst of business matters, and in
times of persecutions and trials, when one can't maintain so much quietude, and in times of dryness, Christ is
a very good friend because we behold Him as a man and
see Him with weaknesses and trials—and He is company for us. Once we have the habit, it is very easy to
find Him present at our side. (L 22.10)

EARTHLY DELIGHT

It is really wonderful to see how the Lord mingles sorrows with joys: that is the straight road which His own
feet trod. (LE 145)

May He be praised for everything. And may He reward
you for the limes: I had been feeling so wretched the
day before they came that I was delighted to have them.
(LE 348)

I have a hermitage which overlooks the river, as the place where I sleep does too, so that I can enjoy the view when I am in bed; and I find that most refreshing. (LE 51)

I am sending you some quinces, which your housekeeper can make into preserves for you to eat as dessert, and also a pot of jam. . . . I do beg you for love of me to eat it all. (LE 101)

The scarcity of fish in this town is so bad that our nuns find it very troublesome. So I was delighted to get this seabream. . . . This is a terrible place when you are not eating meat, for you can never get so much as a fresh egg. (LE 158)

The streets were decorated and there were music, and minstrels, and representatives of the religious orders and nobility such as had never been seen before! . . . Our church was wonderfully adorned with silken hangings, and there were perfumes and colored fountains. One was of orange-flower water and had a very cunning device. There were also some fine altars. A great many salvos of artillery were fired. Such grandeur was a delight to the spirit. (LE 94a)

The patio looked as if it were made of frosted sugar. . . . The garden is most delightful. (LE 94)

It was a great delight for me to consider my soul as a garden and reflect that the Lord was taking His walk in it. (L 14.9)

HUMAN FRIENDSHIP

Since spiritual friendship is so extremely important for souls not yet fortified in virtue—since they have so many opponents and friends to incite them to evil—I don't know how to urge it enough. (L 7.21)

Love alone is what gives value to all things. (S 5.2)

A good means to having God is to speak with His friends, for one always gains very much from this. I know through experience. After the Lord, it is because of persons like these that I am not in hell, for I was always very attached to their praying for me. (W 7.4)

A kiss is a sign of great peace and friendship among two persons. (SS 1.10)

It is a wonderful thing when a sick person finds another wounded with that same sickness; how great the consolation to find you are not alone. The two become a powerful help to each other in suffering and meriting. What excellent backing they give to one another. (L 34.16)

DIVINE FRIENDSHIP

Oh, what a good friend You make, my Lord! (L 8.6)

Love! How I would want to say this word everywhere. . . . He gives us permission to think that He, this true Lover, my Spouse and my Good, needs us. (SS 4.11)

This compassionate Lord . . . desires our friendship. (S 14.3)

He loves whoever loves Him; how good a beloved! O Lord of my soul, who has the words to explain what You give to those who trust in You? (L 22.17)

O my Hope, my Father, my Creator, and my true Lord and Brother! When I consider how You say that Your delights are with the children of men, my soul rejoices greatly. O Lord of heaven and earth . . . what need is there for my love? Why do You want it, my God, or what do You gain? Oh, may You be blessed! (S 7.2)

PRAYER: WATERING A GARDEN

The beginner must realize that to give delight to the Lord, he is starting to cultivate a garden on very barren soil, full of abominable weeds. His Majesty pulls up the weeds and plants good seed. Now let us keep in mind that all of this is already done by the time a soul is determined to practice prayer and has begun to make use of it. And with the help of God, we must strive like good gardeners to get these plants to grow and take pains to water them so that they don't wither but come to bud and flower and give forth a most pleasant fragrance to provide refreshment for this Lord of ours. Then He will often come to take delight in this garden and find His joy among these virtues. (L 11.6)

The garden can be watered in four ways. You may draw water from a well (which is for us a lot of work). Or you may get it by means of a water wheel and aqueducts in such a way that it is obtained by turning the crank of the water wheel. (I have drawn it this way sometimes—the method involves less work than the other, and you get more water.) Or it may flow from a river or a stream. (The garden is watered much better by this means because the ground is more fully soaked, and there is no need to water so frequently—and much less work for the gardener.) Or the water may be provided by a great deal of rain. (For the Lord waters the garden without any work on our part—and this way is incomparably better than all the others mentioned.)

Now, then, these four ways of drawing water to maintain this garden—because without water it will die—are what are important to me and have seemed applicable in explaining the four degrees of prayer. (L 11.7–8)

BEGINNING TO PRAY

Beginners in prayer, we can say, are those who draw water from the well. This involves a lot of work on their own part, as I have said. They must tire themselves in trying to recollect their senses. Since they are accustomed to being distracted, this recollection requires much effort. They need to get accustomed to caring nothing at all about seeing or hearing, to practicing the hours of prayer, and thus to solitude and withdrawal—and to thinking on their past life. (L 11.9)

Take no notice of that feeling you get of wanting to leave off in the middle of your prayer, but praise the Lord for the desire you have to pray: that, you may be sure, comes from your will, which loves to be with God. It is just melancholy that oppresses you and gives you the feeling of constraint. Try occasionally, when you find yourself oppressed in that way, to go to some place where you can see the sky, and walk up and down a little: doing that will not interfere with your prayer, and we must treat this human frailty of ours in such a way that our nature is not subject to undue constraint. (LE 59)

INTERIOR CASTLE

Each one of us has a soul, but since we do not prize souls as is deserved by creatures made in the image of God, we do not understand the deep secrets that lie in them. (IC VII.1.1)

Within us lies something incomparably more precious than what we see outside ourselves. Let's not imagine that we are hollow inside. (W 28.10)

Some books on prayer tell about where one must seek God. Particularly, the glorious St. Augustine speaks about this, for neither in the marketplace nor in pleasures nor anywhere else that he sought God did he find Him as he did when he sought Him within himself. (L 40.6)

The soul is a castle made entirely out of a diamond or a very clear crystal, in which there are many rooms. (IC I.1.1)

Let us imagine that within us is an extremely rich palace, built entirely of gold and precious stones—in sum, built for a lord such as this. Imagine, too, as is indeed so, that you have a part to play in order for the palace to be so beautiful; for there is no edifice as beautiful as is a soul pure and full of virtues. The greater the virtues, the more resplendent the jewels. Imagine, also, that in this palace dwells this mighty King who has been gracious enough to become your Father; and that He is seated upon an extremely valuable throne, which is your heart. (W 28.9)

The things of the soul must always be considered as plentiful, spacious, and large; to do so is not an exaggeration. The soul is capable of much more than we can imagine. (IC I.2.8)

THE PRESENCE OF CHRIST

Though we are always in the presence of God, it seems to me the manner is different with those who practice prayer, for they are aware that He is looking at them. With others, it can happen that several days pass without their recalling that God sees them. (L 8.2)

The soul can place itself in the presence of Christ and grow accustomed to being inflamed with love for His sacred humanity. It can keep Him ever present and speak with Him, asking for its needs and complaining of its labors, being glad with Him in its enjoyments and not forgetting Him because of them, trying to speak to Him, not through written prayers but with words that conform to its desires and needs.

This is an excellent way of making progress, and in a very short time. I consider that soul advanced who strives to remain in this precious company. (L 12.2)

A much greater love for and confidence in this Lord began to develop in me when I saw Him as one with whom I could converse so continually. I saw that He was man, even though He was God. . . . I can speak with Him as with a friend, even though He is Lord. (L 37.5)

Consider the words that divine mouth speaks, for in the first word you will understand immediately the love He has for you; it is no small blessing and gift for the disciple to see that his Master loves him. (W 26.10)

I often consider, my Christ, how pleasing and delightful Your eyes are to one who loves You; and You, my God, want to look with love. It seems to me that only one such gentle glance toward souls that You possess as Yours is enough reward for many years of service. Oh, God help me, how hard it is to explain this unless to those who have already understood how gentle the Lord is! (S 14.1)

This method of keeping Christ present with us is beneficial in all stages and is a very safe means of advancing in the first degree of prayer, of reaching in a short time the second degree. (L 12.3)

3

SETTING OUT *on the* ROAD

THE ROYAL ROAD

They who really love You, my Good, walk safely on a broad and royal road. . . . Hardly have they begun to stumble when You, Lord, give them Your hand. (L 35.14)

I don't see, Lord, nor do I know how the road that leads to You is narrow. I see that it is a royal road, not a path—a road that is safer for anyone who indeed takes it. (L 35.13)

Do not be frightened, daughters, by the many things you need to consider in order to begin this divine journey, which is the royal road to heaven. A great treasure is gained by traveling this road; no wonder we have to pay what seems to us a high price. The time will come when you will understand how trifling everything is next to so precious a reward. (W 21.1)

BEGINNING WELL

Let us deal a little with how this journey must begin; for the beginning is the more important part. (W 20.3)

How they are to begin is very important—in fact, all-important. They must have a great and very resolute determination to persevere until reaching the end, come what may, happen what may, whatever work is involved, whatever criticism arises, whether they arrive or whether they die on the road, or even if they don't have courage for the trials that are met, or if the whole world collapses. (W 20.2)

Many remain at the foot of the mount who could ascend to the top. (SS 2.17)

The Lord told me to get started as best I could, that afterward I would see what His Majesty could do. And how well I have seen it! (L 32.8)

DETERMINATION

Do not stop on the road but, like the strong, fight even to death in the search, for you are not here for any other reason than to fight. You must always proceed with this determination to die rather than fail to reach the end of the journey. (W 20.2)

I marvel at how important it is to be courageous in striving for great things along this path. (L 13.2)

More courage is necessary to follow the path to perfection than to suffer a quick martyrdom. (L 31.17)

Have great confidence, for it is necessary not to hold back one's desires, but to believe in God that if we try we shall little by little, even though it may not be soon, reach the state the saints did with His help. For if they had never determined to desire and seek this state little by little in practice, they would never have mounted so high. His Majesty wants this determination, and He is a friend of courageous souls if they walk in humility and without trusting in self. (L 13.2)

We must be like soldiers who, even though they may not have served a great deal, must always be ready for any duty the captain commands. (W 18.3)

O greatness of God! How You manifest Your power in giving courage to an ant! How true, my Lord, that it is not because of You that those who love You fail to do great works, but because of our own cowardice and pusillanimity. Since we are never determined, but full of human prudence and a thousand fears, You, consequently, my God, do not do your marvelous and great works. Who is more fond than You of giving? (F 2.7)

HOLY DARING

The presumption I would like to see . . . for it always makes humility grow, is to have a holy daring; for God helps the strong, and He shows no partiality. (W 16.2)

It helps a great deal to have lofty thoughts so that we will exert ourselves and make our deeds comply with our thoughts. (W 4.1)

Always have courageous thoughts. As a result of them, the Lord will give you grace for courageous deeds. Believe that these brave thoughts are important. (SS 2.17)

God deliver us, when we do something imperfect, from saying, "We're not angels, we're not saints." Consider that even though we're not, it is a great good to think that if we try we can become saints with God's help. (W 16.2)

NOBLE EFFORT

Oh, I will live in a loftier way. (P 21)

Everything involves struggle before the habit is acquired. (W 29.6)

Nothing is learned without a little effort. . . . If you try . . . within a year, or perhaps half a year, you will acquire it, by the favor of God. See how little time it takes for a gain as great as is that of laying a good foundation. If then the Lord should desire to raise you to higher things, He will discover in you the readiness. (W 29.8)

Once we are determined to undergo this effort, the difficulty passes, for all the pain is but a little in the beginning. (F 14.5)

The Lord doesn't look so much at the greatness of our works as at the love with which they are done. And if we do what we can, His Majesty will enable us each day to do more and more, provided we do not quickly tire. (IC VII.4.15)

SPIRITUAL GUIDANCE

Experience and a spiritual master are necessary, because once the soul has reached these boundaries, many things occur about which it is necessary to have someone to talk to. (L 40.8)

God is very fond of our speaking as truthfully and clearly to the one who stands in His place as we would to Him, and of our desiring that the confessor understand all our thoughts and even more our deeds, however small they be. If you do this, you don't have to go about disturbed or worried. (IC VI.9.12)

It is very important that the master have prudence—I mean that he have good judgment—and experience; if besides these he has learning, so much the better. But if one cannot find these three qualifications together, the first two are more important, since men with a background in studies can be sought out and consulted when there is need. (L 13.6)

Postpone having a master until a suitable person is found, for the Lord will provide one on the condition that all is founded on humility and the desire to do the right thing. (L 13.19)

But souls should be careful that [the master] isn't the kind who will teach them to be toads or who will be satisfied in merely showing them how to catch little lizards. (L 13.3)

If I might have had someone to make me fly, I would have turned desires into deeds more quickly. . . . So few and so rare are the spiritual masters who are not excessively discreet in these matters that I believe it is one of the main reasons why beginners do not advance more rapidly to high perfection. (L 13.6)

I had a confessor who mortified me very much and was sometimes an affliction and great trial to me because he disturbed me exceedingly, and he was the one who profited me the most as far as I can tell. (L 26.3)

Even if the confessor may not be right, she will be more right in not departing from what he tells her, even though it may be an angel of God who speaks to her. . . . For His Majesty will enlighten the confessor or ordain how the task may be carried out. In following the above advice, there is no danger; in doing otherwise, there can be many dangers and much harm. (F 8.5)

READING

My fondness for good books was my salvation. (L 3.7)

In all those years, except for the time after Communion, I never dared to begin prayer without a book. For my soul was as fearful of being without it during prayer as it would have been should it have had to do battle with a lot of people. With this recourse, which was like a partner or a shield by which to sustain the blows of my many thoughts, I went about consoled. For dryness was not usually felt, but it was always felt when I was without a book. Then my soul was thrown into confusion and my thoughts ran wild. With a book I began to collect them, and my soul was drawn to recollection. And many times just opening the book was enough; at other times I read a little, and at others a great deal. (L 4.9)

I have always been fond of the words of the Gospels [that have come from the most sacred mouth in the way

they were said] and found more recollection in them
than in very cleverly written books. (W 21.3)

PRAYER

Don't let anyone deceive you by showing you a road
other than prayer. (W 21.6)

Should anyone tell you that prayer is dangerous, consider him the real danger and run from him. . . . That
the way of prayer be a way of danger—God would
never will that. (W 21.7)

A prayer in which a person is not aware of whom he is
speaking to, what he is asking, who it is who is asking
and of whom, I do not call prayer. . . . Anyone who has
the habit of speaking before God's Majesty as though
he were speaking to a slave, without being careful to see
how he is speaking, but saying whatever comes into his
head and whatever he has learned from saying at other
times, in my opinion is not praying. (IC I.1.7)

HOW TO PRAY

May God deliver us from foolish devotions. (L 13.16)

This is the method of prayer that I then used: since I
could not reflect discursively with the intellect, I strove
to picture Christ within me, and it did me greater
good—in my opinion—to picture Him in those scenes
where I saw Him more alone. It seemed to me that being
alone and afflicted, as a person in need, He had to accept

me. . . . I remained with Him as long as my thoughts allowed me to, for there were many distractions that tormented me. (L 9.4)

I had such little ability to represent things with my intellect that if I hadn't seen the things, my imagination was not of use to me, as it was to other persons who can imagine things and thus recollect themselves. I could only think about Christ as He was as man. . . . This was the reason I liked images so much. (L 9.6)

LOOK AT HIM

Let us begin to think about an episode of the Passion, let's say of when our Lord was bound to the pillar. The intellect goes in search of reasons for better understanding the great sorrows and pain His Majesty suffered in that solitude and many other things that the intellect, if it works hard, can herein deduce. How much more if it is the intellect of a learned man! This is the method of prayer with which all must begin, continue, and finish; and it is a very excellent and safe path until the Lord leads one to other supernatural things. . . . But one should not always weary oneself in seeking these reflections but just remain there in His presence with the intellect quiet. If a person is able, he should occupy himself in looking at Christ who is looking at him. (L 13.12, 22)

Those of you who cannot engage in much discursive reflection with the intellect or keep your mind from distraction, get used to this practice! Get used to it! See, I know that you can do this; for I suffered many years from the trial—and it is a very great one—of not being able to quiet the mind in anything. But I know that the Lord does not leave us so abandoned; for if we humbly ask Him for this friendship, He will not deny it to us. And if we cannot succeed in one year, we will succeed later. Let's not regret the time that is so well spent. Who's making us hurry? (W 26.2)

THE CROSS

It is an important matter for beginners in prayer to start off by becoming detached from every kind of satisfaction and to enter the path solely with the determination to help Christ carry the cross like good cavaliers, who desire to serve their king at no salary since their salary is certain. We should fix our eyes on the true and everlasting kingdom that we are trying to gain. (L 15.11)

Begin with the determination to follow the way of the cross and not desire consolations, since the Lord Himself pointed out this way of perfection, saying: *Take up your cross and follow Me.* He is our model; whoever follows His counsels solely for the sake of pleasing Him has nothing to fear. (L 15.13)

There are many who begin, yet they never reach the end. I believe this is mainly because of failure to embrace the cross from the beginning. (L 11.15)

The greatest labor is in the beginning, because it is the beginner who works while the Lord gives the increase. In the other degrees of prayer, the greatest thing is enjoying; although whether in the beginning, the middle, or the end, all bear their crosses even though these crosses be different. For all who follow Christ, if they don't want to get lost, must walk along this path that He trod. And blessed be the trials that even here in this life are so superabundantly repaid. (L 11.5)

MANY PATHS

God doesn't lead all by one path, and perhaps the one who thinks she is walking along a very lowly path is in fact higher in the eyes of the Lord. (W 17.2)

There are many souls that benefit more by other meditations than those on the sacred Passion. For just as there are many mansions in heaven, there are many paths. Some persons find it helpful to think about hell, others about death; some, if they have tender hearts, experience much fatigue if they always think about the Passion, and they are refreshed and helped by considering the power and grandeur of God in creatures—and the love He bore us, and its manifestation in all things. This is an admirable method of procedure as long as one often reflects on the Passion and life of Christ, from which has come and continues to come every good. (L 13.13)

Let us believe that all is for our own greater good. Let His Majesty lead the way along the path He desires. We belong no longer to ourselves but to Him. (L 11.2)

4

HARD WORK
and
VIRTUE

CONCERN FOR OTHERS

Let's not think that everything is accomplished through much weeping but set our hands to the task of hard work and virtue. (IC VI.6.9)

The Lord asks of us only two things: love of His Majesty and love of our neighbor. (IC V.3.7)

We cannot know whether or not we love God, although there are strong indications for recognizing that we do love Him; but we can know whether we love our neighbor. And be certain that the more advanced you see you are in love for your neighbor, the more advanced you will be in the love of God. (IC V.3.8)

Sympathize with your neighbor in his trials, however small they may be. (W 7.6)

Another very good proof of love is that you strive in household duties to relieve others of work, and also rejoice and praise the Lord very much for any increase you see in their virtues. (W 7.9)

Works are what the Lord wants! He desires that if you see a Sister who is sick to whom you can bring some relief, you have compassion on her and not worry about losing this devotion; and that if she is suffering pain, you also feel it. (IC V.3.11)

Love is always stirring and thinking about what it will do. It cannot contain itself. (L 30.19)

Force your will to do the will of your Sisters in everything, even though you may lose your rights; forget your own good for their sakes no matter how much resistance your nature puts up; and, when the occasion arises, strive to accept work yourself so as to relieve your neighbor of it. Don't think that it won't cost you anything or that you will find everything done for you. Look at what our Spouse's love for us cost Him. (IC V.3.12)

Love begets love. Even if we are at the very beginning and are very wretched, let us strive to keep this divine love always before our eyes and to waken ourselves to love. (L 22.14)

There is nothing annoying that is not suffered easily by those who love one another. (W 4.5)

All must be friends, all must be loved, all must be held dear. (W 4.7)

EGO ANNIHILATION

Doing our own will is usually what harms us. (IC III.2.12)

So, let us try hard to go against our own will in everything. . . . But how extremely rigorous, it seems, to say that we shouldn't please ourselves in anything, when we do not also mention the pleasure and delight this going against our will carries in its wake, and what is gained by it even in this life. (W 12.3)

This interior mortification is acquired . . . by proceeding gradually, not giving in to our own will and appetites, even in little things, until the body is completely surrendered to the spirit. . . . The whole matter, or a great part of it, lies in losing concern about ourselves and our own satisfaction. (W 12.1–2)

Although interiorly it takes time to become totally detached and mortified, exteriorly it must be done immediately. (W 13.7)

Let us strive always to look at virtues and good deeds we see in others and cover their defects with the thought of our own great sins. This is a manner of acting that, although we cannot do so with perfection right away, gradually gains for us a great virtue—that is, considering all others better than ourselves. (L 13.10)

GOD'S WILL

The whole aim of any person who is beginning prayer—and don't forget this, because it's very important—should be that he work and prepare himself with determination and every possible effort to bring his will into conformity with God's will. Be certain that, as I shall say later, the greatest perfection attainable along the spiritual path lies in this conformity. It is the person who lives in more perfect conformity who will receive more from the Lord and be more advanced on this road. Don't think that in what concerns perfection there is some mystery or things unknown or things to be still understood, for in perfect conformity to God's will lies all our good. (IC II.1.8)

This union with God's will is the union I have desired all my life; it is the union I ask the Lord for always and the one that is clearest and safest. (IC V.3.5)

His will must be done whether we like this or not. . . . Believe me, take my advice, and make a virtue of necessity. (W 32.4)

OBEDIENCE

Study diligently how to be prompt in obedience. (IC III.2.12)

I have seen through experience the great good that comes to a soul when it does not turn aside from obedience. It is through this practice that I think one advances in virtue and gains humility. . . . Those restless stirrings within us, which make us fond of doing our own will, and which even subdue reason in matters concerning our own satisfaction, come to a stop. (F P.1)

Strive to obey, even if this may be more painful for you, since the greatest perfection lies in obedience. (W 39.3)

Obedience gives strength. (F P.2)

TRUST

Oh, oh, oh, how little we trust You, Lord! (S 13.3)

Carefully avoid wasting your thoughts at any time on what you will eat. Let the body work, for it is good that you work to sustain yourselves; let your soul be at rest. Leave this care, as has been amply pointed out, to your Spouse; He will care for you always. (W 34.4)

So, let's not complain of fears or become discouraged at seeing our nature weak and without strength. Let us strive to strengthen ourselves with humility and understand clearly the little we ourselves can do, and that if God does not favor us, we are nothing. Let us distrust completely our own strength and confide in His Mercy, and until we attain this mercy, our weakness will persist. (SS 3.12)

One day while I was anxiously desiring to help the order, the Lord told me: "Do what lies in your power; surrender yourself to me, and do not be disturbed about anything." (T 10)

The safest way is to want only what God wants. He knows more than we ourselves do, and He loves us. Let us place ourselves in His hands. (IC VI.9.16)

When the Lord gives us such a multitude of trials to bear all at once, He always gives us some good things as well, for, knowing how weak we are, He tempers our sufferings to our strength, and does everything for our good. (LE 210)

When things seem to be going best, I am generally less happy about them than I am now. You know the Lord always wants us to realize that it is His Majesty Himself Who does what is good for us. And He often allows us to suffer trial upon trial so that we may realize this better and recognize that it is His doing. Those are the times when everything goes off best. (LE 148)

Let us try hard, let us trust hard. (S 14.13)

HUMILITY

This whole groundwork of prayer is based on humility. The more a soul lowers itself in prayer, the more God raises it up. I don't recall His ever having granted me one of the very notable favors of which I shall speak later if not at a time when I was brought to nothing at the sight of my wretchedness. (L 22.11)

Humility is a mirror in which we see how none of our good deeds has its principle from ourselves. . . . In doing anything good or seeing it done, we must give heed to the source and understand how without this help we can do nothing. We must begin immediately to thank God and not think of ourselves in anything good that we do. (IC I.2.5)

Humility does not disturb or disquiet or agitate, however great it may be; it comes with peace, delight, and calm. (W 39.2)

I wouldn't want this to be forgotten: In this life the soul doesn't grow like the body, even though we say it grows—and in fact it does. After a child grows up and develops a strong body and becomes an adult, the child's body doesn't dwindle and grow small again. But in the case of the soul, the Lord desires this to happen. . . . The purpose must be to humiliate us for our own great good and so that we might not become careless while in this exile. (L 15.12)

There is no need to go dredging up things in order to derive some humility and shame, because the Lord Himself gives this prayer in a manner very different from that which we gain through our nice little reasonings. For such humility is nothing in comparison with the true humility the Lord with His light here teaches and that causes an embarrassment that undoes one. (L 15.14)

Humility! Humility! By this means the Lord allows Himself to be conquered with regard to anything we want from Him. The first sign for seeing whether or not you have humility is that you do not think you deserve these favors and spiritual delights from the Lord or that you will receive them in your lifetime. (IC IV.2.9)

Believe me, in the presence of infinite Wisdom, a little study of humility and one act of humility is worth more than all the knowledge of the world. (L 15.8)

HUMOR

I laugh at myself. (L 30.20)

These affairs of ours do teach us what the world is like: really, it is as good as a play! (LE 171)

Some persons came to me with great fear to tell me we were in trouble and that it could happen that others might accuse me of something and report me to the Inquisitors. This amused me and made me laugh. (L 33.5)

I made fun of myself. (L 30.20)

I am being a stumbling block and getting in everybody's way . . . perhaps the solution would be to throw me into the sea. (LE 214)

I was sorry to hear of the distress our affairs are causing you, but I must tell you I do not take them so tragically myself, for I know they are in the hands of God and are His Majesty's business more than ours. So, whatever happens, I shall be content. . . . I received the letter . . . it was so apprehensive that it made me laugh. (LE 267)

It makes me laugh to think how you send me sweets and presents and money, and I send you hair shirts! (LE 163)

Blessed be God, we shall find no changes of weather in eternity. (LE 34)

COMMON SENSE

See that both spiritual and temporal needs are provided for; and these things should be done with a mother's love. (CO 34)

It seems an inappropriate thing to begin with temporal matters. Yet I think that these are most important for the promotion of the spiritual good. . . . It is necessary to have good order and attend to matters concerning

government and the harmonious organization of everything. (VI 2)

Even in good things we need rule and measure, so as
not to ruin our health and become incapable of enjoying
them. (F 6.7)

There are many reasons why it is permitted to take recreation—even so as to be able to return with greater
strength to prayer. (L 13.1)

What I said to him most emphatically was that he
should see they were given good food. (LE 148)

The fact that something is a novelty is reason enough
for not starting it. (VI 24)

You cannot regulate all souls by the same yardstick.
(LE 184)

The soul should be led gently. (LE 59)

I like to lay great stress on the virtues, but not on austerity. (LE 148)

Discretion is very necessary in all. (W 19.13)

5

BRAVADO
and
BEYOND

CHEAP TALK

How is it that you want to please Him only with words? (IC VII.4.8)

The love we have for Him . . . must not be fabricated in our imaginations but proved by deeds. . . . He needs the determination of our wills. (IC III.1.7)

I'm not good at anything but talk, and so You don't desire, my God, to put me to work; everything adds up to just words and desires about how much I must serve. . . . Ordain ways in which I might do something for You, for there is no longer anyone who can suffer to receive so much and not repay anything. Cost what it may, Lord, do not desire that I come into Your presence with hands so empty. (L 21.5)

If you love Him, strive that what you say to the Lord may not amount to mere polite words; strive to suffer what His Majesty desires you to suffer. For, otherwise, when you give your will, it would be like showing a jewel to another, making a gesture to give it away, and asking that he take it; but when he extends his hand to accept it, you pull yours back and hold on tightly to the jewel. . . . Let's give Him the jewel once and for all. (W 32.7–8)

Our deeds show that these are not merely polite words. (W 32.12)

If we don't advance, let us walk with great fear. . . . Love is never idle, and a failure to grow would be a very bad sign. A soul that has tried to be the betrothed of God Himself, that is now intimate with His Majesty . . . must not go to sleep. (IC V.4.10)

Perfection as well as its reward does not consist in spiritual delights, but in greater love and in deeds done with greater justice and truth. (IC III.2.10)

It is love's nature to serve with deeds in a thousand ways. (IC VI.9.18)

FRAGMENTATION

I was living an extremely burdensome life, because in prayer I understood more clearly my faults. On the one hand, God was calling me; on the other hand, I was following the world. All the things of God made me happy; those of the world held me bound. It seems I desired to harmonize these two contraries—so inimical to one another—such as are the spiritual life and sensory joys, pleasures, and pastimes. In prayer I was having great trouble, for my spirit was not proceeding as lord but as slave. And so I was not able to shut myself within myself (which was my whole manner of procedure in prayer); instead, I shut within myself a thousand vanities.

Thus I passed many years, for now I am surprised how I could have put up with both and not abandon either the one or the other. (L 7.17)

I voyaged on this tempestuous sea for almost twenty years with these fallings and risings. . . . It is one of the most painful lives that one can imagine; for neither did I enjoy God, nor did I find happiness in the world. When I was experiencing the enjoyments of the world, I felt sorrow when I recalled what I owed to God. When I was with God, my attachments to the world disturbed me. This is a war so troublesome that I don't know how I was able to suffer it even for a month, much less for so many years. (L 8.2)

What hope can we have of finding rest outside of ourselves if we cannot be at rest within? (IC II.1.9)

All the contempt and trials one can endure in this life cannot be compared to these interior battles. Any disquiet and war can be suffered if we find peace where we live, as I have already said. But that we desire to rest from the thousand trials there are in the world, and that the Lord wants to prepare us for tranquillity, and that within ourselves lies the obstacle to such rest and tranquillity, cannot fail to be very painful and almost unbearable. (IC IV.1.12)

DOWNFALLS

If we were to look at nothing else but the way, we would soon arrive. But we meet with a thousand falls and obstacles and lose the way because we don't keep our eyes—as I say—on the true way. (W 16.11)

If there is going to be a downfall, it's better that it happen in the beginning rather than later. (IC V.4.8)

I write this for the consolation of the weak souls like myself, that they might never despair or fail to trust in the greatness of God. Even though they may fall after elevations like the ones to which the Lord here brings them, they ought not to grow discouraged if they don't want to become completely lost. (L 19.3)

If you should at times fall, don't become discouraged and stop striving to advance. For even from this fall God will draw out good, as does the seller of an antidote who drinks some poison to test whether his antidote is effective. (IC II.1.9)

Here, my daughters, is where love will be seen: not hidden in corners, but in the midst of the occasions of falling. And believe me that even though there may be more faults, and even some slight losses, our gain will be incomparably greater. (F 5.15)

There will always be failures as long as we live in this mortal body. (IC VI.7.4)

PRESUMPTION

They pay little attention to small matters and hence come to fall in very great ones. (VI 21)

The virtues are not yet strong, nor does [the soul] have the experience to recognize dangers, nor does it know the harm done by relying upon oneself. (L 19.14)

What a strange belief it is, that the toad should expect to fly of itself whenever it wants. And it seems to me to be even more difficult and troublesome for our spirit to raise itself up if God doesn't raise it, for it is weighted down with the earth and a thousand obstacles, and wanting to fly profits it little. Although flying is more natural to it than to the toad, it is so bogged down in the mud that through its own fault it lost this ability. (L 22.13)

Let us leave it to the Lord. (For He knows us better than we do ourselves. And true humility is content with what is received.) There are some persons who demand favors from God as though these were due them in justice. That's a nice kind of humility! Thus, He who knows all very seldom grants such persons favors, and rightly so. He sees clearly that they are not ready to drink from the chalice. (W 18.6)

SELF-KNOWLEDGE

Another dangerous temptation: self-assurance in the thought that we will in no way return to our past faults and worldly pleasures. . . . If this self-assurance is present in beginners, it is very dangerous because with it a person doesn't take care . . . and he falls flat; please God, the relapse will not bring something much worse. . . . Never proceed with such self-assurance that you stop fearing lest you fall again. . . . However sublime the contemplation, let your prayer always begin and end with self-knowledge. (W 39.4–5)

Knowing ourselves is something so important that I wouldn't want any relaxation ever in this regard, however high you may have climbed into the heavens. While we are on this earth, nothing is more important to us than humility. . . . Let's strive to make more progress in self-knowledge. In my opinion, we shall never completely know ourselves if we don't strive to know God. By gazing at His grandeur, we get in touch with our own lowliness; by looking at His purity, we shall see our own filth; by pondering His humility, we shall see how far we are from being humble. (IC I.2.9)

CARELESSNESS AND COMPLACENCY

In our human nature, custom is a terrible thing, and little by little, through small things, irremediable harm is done. (VI 5)

When the Lord truly gives one of these solid virtues, it seems it carries all the others in its wake. The truly humble person always walks in doubt about his own virtues, and usually those he sees in his neighbors seem more certain and valuable. (W 38.9)

Be careful and attentive—this is very important—until you see that you are strongly determined not to offend the Lord. . . . There is nothing small if it goes against His immense Majesty. . . . It's serious, very serious. (W 41.3)

The soul here resembles someone on a journey who enters a quagmire or swamp and thus cannot move onward. And, in order to advance, a soul must not only walk but fly. (F 6.15)

Do not feel secure or let yourself go to sleep! By feeling secure, you would resemble someone who very tranquilly lies down after having locked his doors for fear of thieves while allowing the thieves to remain inside the house. And you already know that there is no worse thief than we ourselves. (W 10.1)

The one among you who feels safest should fear more. (IC VII.4.3)

Consider that through very little things the door is opened to very big things, and that without your realizing it, the world will start entering your lives. (F 27.11)

VIGILANCE

You must always proceed carefully and turn away from every occasion and companion who does not help you come closer to God. We should take great care in everything we do to bend our will, and take care that our speech is edifying; we must flee those places where conversations are not of God. (W 41.4)

Don't think, even though it may seem to you, that virtue has already been gained if it hasn't been tried by its contrary. We must always be mistrustful of ourselves and never grow negligent as long as we live. . . . In this life there is never anything that hasn't any dangers. (L 31.19)

The one who goes highest must fear the most and trust less in self. (L 15.2)

What His Majesty gave us are love and fear. Love will quicken our steps; fear will make us watch our steps to avoid falling along the way. On this way, there are many stumbling blocks for all of us who are alive and continue our journey. With this fear we will be secure against being deceived. . . . Love and fear of God: what more could you ask for! They are like two fortified castles from which one can wage war on the world and the devils. (W 40.1–2)

PERSEVERANCE

God does not deny Himself to anyone who perseveres. Little by little, He will measure out the courage sufficient to attain victory. (L 11.4)

Do not stop short on the road but try hard until you reach the end. (W 25.4)

Unhappy [the soul] will be if it turns back. I think turning back would mean falling to the bottom. (L 15.2)

There is no reason to stop in the middle. (L 16.8)

Perseverance is most necessary here. One always gains much through perseverance. (IC II.1.3)

My desire is not powerful, my God; You are the powerful One. What I can do is be determined; thus from this very moment I am determined to serve You through deeds. (SS 4.12)

COURAGE

I would not want you to be womanish in anything, nor would I want you to be like women but like strong men.

For if you do what lies in your power, the Lord will make you so strong that you will astonish men. (W 7.8)

If trials are suffered for Him, His Majesty adapts them to our strength. Thus, if we are so afraid of them, it is because we are fainthearted and miserable. (SS 4.7)

If you always ask God to foster this way of life and you trust not at all in yourselves, He will not deny you His mercy. And if you have confidence in Him and have courageous spirits—for His Majesty is very fond of these— you need not fear that He will fail you in anything. (F 27.12)

SPIRITUAL WARFARE

There must be war in this life. In the face of so many enemies, it's not possible for us to sit with our hands folded; there must always be this care about how we are proceeding interiorly and exteriorly. (SS 2.2)

Let the soul be manly and . . . determined to fight . . . and realize that there are no better weapons than those of the cross. (IC II.1.6)

You should never let a word of praise pass without it moving you to wage war interiorly, for this is easily done if you acquire the habit. . . . Stand here with a sword in the hand of your thoughts. Although you think the praise does you no harm, do not trust it. (SS 2.12)

It's impossible for us to be angels here below because such is not our nature. In fact, a soul doesn't disturb me when I see it with great temptations. If love and fear of our Lord are present, the soul will gain very much; I'm certain of that. If I see a soul always quiet and without any war—for I've run into some like this—I always fear even if I do not see it offending the Lord. . . . To be without war is impossible. (SS 2.3)

> Oh, you cowards, see
> This little maid
> Who values not gold
> Nor her beauty admires.
> She embraces the war
> And persecution endures
> To suffer bravely
> With heart truly great. (P 23)

> O fortunate this war!
> Not one coward will there be!
> Let us risk our lives!
> None better guards it
> Than he who loses it.
> Our guide is Jesus,
> The reward of this warring.
> *Sleep no longer, sleep no more,*
> *For there is no peace on earth.* (P 29)

EYES ON CHRIST

Life is long, and there are in it many trials, and we need to look at Christ our model, how He suffered them, and also at His apostles and saints, so as to bear these trials with perfection. Jesus is too good a companion for us to turn away from Him. (IC VI.7.13)

Fix your eyes on the Crucified and everything will become small for you. (IC VII.4.8)

All harm comes to us from not keeping our eyes fixed on You. (W 16.11)

In seeing You at my side, I saw all blessings. There is no trial that it wasn't good for me to suffer once I looked at You as You were, standing before the judges. Whoever lives in the presence of so good a friend and excellent a leader, who went ahead of us to be the first to suffer, can endure all things. The Lord helps us, strengthens us, and never fails; He is a true friend. (L 22.6)

You say that Your delight is to be with the children of men. O my Lord! What is this? As often as I hear these words, they bring me great consolation; they did so even when I was very far gone. (L 14.10)

≽ 6 ≼

MISTAKES, RUTS, *and* ROADBLOCKS

SELFISHNESS

How little we understand ourselves! There is a bit of self-love in everything we do. (LE 289)

The ways of this world are quite beyond me: as soon as self-interest enters into a thing, sanctity is forgotten, and that makes me feel that I loathe the whole business. (LE 154)

The more goods people possess, the greater the tedium. (F 10.9)

O selfish people, greedy for your pleasures and delights, not waiting a short time to enjoy them in such abundance, not waiting a year, not waiting a day, not waiting an hour—and perhaps it will take no more than a moment—you lose everything. (S 13.2)

Be aware that, without understanding how, you will find yourselves so attached that you will be unable to manage the attachment. Oh, God help me, the silly things that come from such attachments are too numerous to be counted. (W 4.8)

If we tell a rich person living in luxury that it is God's will that he be careful and use moderation at table so that others might at least have bread to eat, for they are dying of hunger, he will bring up a thousand reasons for not understanding this save in accordance with his own selfish purposes. If we tell a backbiter that it is God's will that he love his neighbor as himself, he will become impatient and no reason will suffice to make him understand. We can tell a religious who has grown accustomed to his freedom and comfort that he should remember his obligation to give good example and keep in mind that when he says these words, they are not just words but are to be put into practice . . . but it is just useless to insist nowadays with some of them. (W 33.1)

SELF-INDULGENCE

Who has told us that comfortable living is good? What is this, that some persons spend their days eating well and sleeping and seeking recreations and all the rest they can? (SS 2.14)

A fault this body has is that the more comfort we try to give it, the more needs it discovers. It's amazing how much comfort it wants. (W 11.2)

The body grows fat and the soul weakens. We must not find our rest in being lax, but must test ourselves sometimes. I know that this flesh is very deceptive and that we need to understand it. (SS 2.15)

Once we start worrying about our bodily needs, those of the soul will be forgotten. (W 34.2)

We have such stingy hearts that it seems to us we're going to lose the earth if we desire to neglect the body a little for the sake of the spirit. . . . It makes me sad that we have so little confidence in God and so much self-love. (L 13.4)

When we begin to conquer these wretched little bodies, we will not be so troubled by them. . . . If we do not determine once and for all to swallow death and the lack of health, we will never do anything. (W 11.4)

FUSS

I thought I would be able to serve God much better if I were in good health. This is our mistake: not abandoning ourselves entirely to what the Lord does, for He knows best what is fitting for us. (L 6.5)

You say: *Come to me all who labor and are burdened, for I will comfort you.* What more do we want, Lord? What are we asking for? What do we seek? Why are those in the world so unhappy if not because of seeking rest? God help me! Oh, God help me! What is this, Lord? Oh, what a pity! Oh, what a great blindness, that we seek rest where it is impossible to find it! (S 8.2)

They have their times for prayer. Our Lord gives them tenderness and tears. Yet, they do not want to give up the enjoyments of this life. They want to live a good and well-ordered life, for they think it is beneficial for them to live here below in tranquility. Life bears with it many changes. They will be doing enough if they continue in the practice of virtue. But if they don't withdraw from the pleasures and satisfactions of the world, they will soon grow lax in walking the Lord's path. (SS 2.22)

FAMILY SYSTEMS

I am astonished by the harm that is caused by dealing with relatives. (W 9.2)

We are living in such miserable times and our nature is so weak that we don't want to offend relatives. (W 14.3)

Relatives tire me very much. (T 2.6)

I have been much loved by my relatives—according to what they have said—and I loved them so much that I didn't let them forget me. But I know through my own experience, as well as that of others, that in time of trial my relatives helped me least. It was the servants of God who helped me. By relatives I do not mean parents, for parents very seldom fail to help their children, and it is right for us to console them in their need. Let us not remain aloof from them. (W 9.3)

Believe that you can trust those who love you only for His sake more than you can all your relatives, and that these former will not fail you. And you will find fathers and brothers in those about whom you had not even thought. For since these seek to be repaid by God, they do things for us. Those who seek to be repaid by us soon grow tired. (W 9.4)

It seemed to me a few years ago not only that I was detached from my relatives but that they bored me; so I felt certain that I couldn't bear their conversation. A very important business matter came about, and I had to stay with my sister, whom I previously loved very much. . . . I saw that her troubles grieved me and worried me more than would those of a neighbor. In the end, I understood I wasn't as free as I thought. (L 31.19)

INANE CONVERSATION

For the love of God, I beg you that your conversation always be directed toward bringing some good to the one with whom you are speaking. (W 20.3)

If I speak or have dealings with some secular persons because matters can't be otherwise, and even though the subject may concern prayer, I find that if the conversation is prolonged, just a diversion and unnecessary, I am forcing myself to continue, because such conversation is a severe hardship for me. (T 1.2)

God is your business and language. Whoever wants to speak to you must learn this language; and if he doesn't, be on your guard that you don't learn his; it will be a hell. (W 20.4)

For many years I took part in this noxious form of recreation. (L 7.7)

If no effort is being made to make the conversation a fruitful one, they should bring it to a quick conclusion. (CO 18)

There's no longer time for children's games, for these worldly friendships, even though they may be good,

seem to be nothing else. Unless there is a very good reason and it is for the benefit of that soul, don't let your
conversation be of the sort in which you ask, "Do you
like me?" or "Don't you like me?" (W 20.4)

DISPERSION

You are in that Babylon, where you will always hear
things tending rather to diversion than to recollection.
(LE 249)

I thus began to go from pastime to pastime, from vanity
to vanity, from one occasion to another, to place myself
often in very serious occasions, and to allow my soul to
become spoiled by many vanities. (L 7.1)

Since I wasted time on other vanities, I cared little about
losing time. (L 7.13)

He is the friend of all good order. Now, then, if we fill
the palace with lowly people and trifles, how will there
be room for the Lord with His court? He does enough
by remaining just a little while in the midst of so much
confusion. (W 28.12)

COMPULSIVE BUSINESS

Even though they are very involved in the world, they
have good desires, and sometimes, though only once in
a while, they entrust themselves to our Lord and reflect
on who they are, although in a rather hurried fashion.
During the period of a month they will sometimes pray,

but their minds are then filled with business matters that ordinarily occupy them. They are so attached to these things that where their treasure lies, their heart goes also. Sometimes they do put all these things aside, and the self-knowledge and awareness that they are not proceeding correctly in order to get to the door is important. Finally, they enter the first, lower rooms. But so many reptiles get in with them that they are prevented from seeing the beauty of the castle and from calming down. (IC I.1.8)

It's as if a person were to enter a place where the sun is shining but be hardly able to open his eyes because of the mud in them. The room is bright, but he doesn't enjoy it because of the impediment of things like these wild animals or beasts that make him close his eyes to everything but them. So, I think, must be the condition of the soul. Even though it may not be in a bad state, it is so involved in worldly affairs and so absorbed with its possessions, honor, or business affairs, that even though as a matter of fact it would want to see and enjoy its beauty, these things do not allow it to; nor does it seem that it can slip free from so many impediments. If a person is to enter the second dwelling place, it is important that he strive to give up unnecessary things and business affairs. Each one should do this in conformity with his state in life. (IC I.1.2)

MONEY AND PRESTIGE

I laugh at and am even distressed about the things they come here to ask us to pray for: to ask His Majesty for wealth and money. . . . No, my Sisters, this is not the time to be discussing with God matters that have little importance. (W 1.5)

Oh, as for riches! If people have easily what they need and a lot of money in their coffers and guard against committing serious sins, they think everything is done. They enjoy what they have. They give alms from time to time. They do not reflect that their own riches are not their own but given by the Lord so that they, as His stewards, may share their wealth among the poor, and that they must give strict account for the time they keep surplus supply in their coffers while delaying and putting off the poor who are suffering. . . . Beg the Lord to give rich people light, that they may not continue in this daze. (SS 2.8)

It is not money that will sustain us but faith, perfection, and trust in God alone. (CO 21)

[Spiritually serious persons] know very well that they would bring about more good in one day than they would in ten years if, for the love of God, they thought a lot less of the prestige of their office. (L 21.9)

We love ourselves very much; there's an extraordinary amount of prudence we use so not to lose our rights. Oh, what a great deception! May the Lord through His mercy enlighten us so that we do not fall into similar darkness. (IC V.4.6)

HUMAN APPROVAL

What difference does it make what others think? (IC VI.4.16)

If we are always fixed on our earthly misery, the stream will never flow free from the mud of fear, faintheartedness, and cowardice. I would be looking to see if I'm being watched or not, [or] if, by taking this path, things will turn out badly for me . . . [or] whether I might be judged better than others if I don't follow the path they all do. (IC I.2.10)

Give up these fears; never pay attention in like matters to the opinion of the crowd. (W 21.10)

Never does the world exalt without putting down. . . . I have a lot of experience of this. It used to afflict me to see so much blindness in these praises, and now I laugh at myself as though someone crazy were speaking. Remember your sins, and if in some matters people speak the truth praising you, note that the virtue is not yours and that you are obliged to serve more. Awaken fear in your soul so that you do not rest in the kiss of this false peace given by the world; think that it is a kiss from Judas. (SS 2.13)

[Some spiritual persons] are too attached to their honor. They would not want to do anything that was not really acceptable to men as well as to the Lord; . . . the trouble is that without one's being aware of it, the interests of the world almost always gain more than do those of God. These souls, for the most part, grieve over anything said against them. (SS 2.26)

There is nothing so small in which there is so obvious a danger as this concern about honor and whether we have been offended. (W 12.8)

WORKAHOLISM

You are not made of iron. . . . Many good brains have been ruined through overwork. (LE 160)

For the love of God, reduce the amount of work you are doing, or else, if you do not [do this] in time, you will find the trouble is beyond cure. Learn to master yourself, and take yourself in hand. (LE 290)

Anyone who works all the year round badly needs relaxation. (LE 236)

ABANDONING PRAYER

Prayer is an exercise of love, and it would be incorrect to think that if there were no time for solitude, there would be no prayer at all. (L 7.12)

No sooner does our head begin to ache than we stop going to [prayer], which won't kill us either. We stay away one day because our head ached, another because it was just now aching, and three more so it won't ache again. (W 10.6)

I abandoned [prayer] for a year and a half. . . . And doing this was no more, nor could it have been, than putting myself right in hell. (L 19.4)

What terrible blindness mine was. . . . What folly: to flee from the light so as to be always stumbling! . . . To give up the practice of prayer was the greatest evil. (L 19.10)

During the time in which I was without prayer, my life was much worse. (L 19.11)

If they don't return to prayer, they will go from bad to worse. . . . What I advise strongly is not to abandon prayer, for in prayer a person will understand what he is doing and win fortitude to lift himself up. And you must believe that if you give up prayer, you are, in my opinion, courting danger. (L 15.3)

7

DISILLUSIONMENT

DISCOURAGEMENT

My life has been so wretched that I have not found a saint among those who were converted to God in whom I can find comfort. For I note that after the Lord called them, they did not turn back and offend Him. As for me, not only did I turn back and become worse, but it seems I made a study out of resisting the favors His Majesty was granting me. (L P.1)

It is a shame and unfortunate that through our own fault we don't understand ourselves or know who we are. (IC I.1.2)

It is good to walk in fear of self so as to avoid trusting oneself either little or much. . . . Always, as long as we live, even for the sake of humility, it is good to know our miserable nature. (L 13.1)

Our nature is so dead that we go after what we see in the present. (L 10.6)

Our natural bent is toward the worst rather than toward the best. (L 2.3)

Our human nature often asks for more than what it needs. (CO 22)

Since we are the way we are, inclined to base things and with so little love and courage, it was necessary for us to see His love and courage to be awakened—and not just once but every day. (W 33.2)

SELF-KNOWLEDGE

I consider one day of humble self-knowledge a greater favor from the Lord, even though the day may have cost us numerous afflictions and trials, than many days of prayer. (F 5.16)

The soul is like water in a glass: the water looks very clear if the sun doesn't shine on it; but when the sun shines on it, it seems to be full of dust particles. This comparison is an exact one. Before being in this ecstasy, the soul thinks it is careful about not offending God and that it is doing what it can in conformity with its own strength. But once it is brought into prayer, which this Sun of justice bestows on it and which opens its eyes, it sees so many dust particles that it would want to close its eyes again. It is not yet so much a child of this powerful eagle that it can gaze steadily at this sun. But for the little time that it holds its eyes open, it sees that it is itself filled with mud. (L 20.28)

IMPERMANENCE

What little security we have while living in this exile. (IC III.1.1)

In this life, we cannot always be in a stable condition. (L 40.18)

How quickly all things come to an end. (W 29.1)

Now it seems to me that those whom God brings to a certain clear knowledge love very differently than do those who have not reached it. This clear knowledge is about the nature of the world, that there is another world, about the difference between the one and the other, that the one is eternal and the other a dream; or about the nature of loving the Creator and loving the creature. (W 6.3)

Bear in mind continually how all is vanity and how quickly everything comes to an end. This helps remove our attachment to trivia and center it on what will never end. (W 10.2)

MENDACITY

All things we pay attention to here below are lies and jokes. (W 34.9)

After all, the world is the world. (W 9.4)

All earthly life is filled with deception and duplicity: when you think you have won a friend, according to what is shown you, you afterward come to understand that was all a lie. It isn't possible anymore to live in the midst of such intrigue, [which is] especially present where there is something to be gained. (L 21.1)

So goes this world; it would clearly show us its frenzy if we were not blind. (F 10.3)

I'm not merely saying that we should not tell lies. . . . I'm saying that we should walk in truth before God and people in as many ways as possible. Especially, there should be no desire that others consider us better than we are. (IC VI.10.6)

God is supreme Truth; and to be humble is to walk in truth, for it is a very deep truth that of ourselves we have nothing good but only misery and nothingness. Whoever does not understand this walks in falsehood. (IC VI.10.7)

PHYSICAL LIMITATIONS

We are so miserable that our poor little imprisoned soul shares in the miseries of the body; the changes in the weather and the rotating of the bodily humors often have the result that without their fault, souls cannot do what they desire, but suffer in every way. . . . It is a great misfortune to a soul that loves God to see that it lives in this misery and cannot do what it desires because it has as wretched a guest as is this body. (L 11.15)

Oh, how painful it is for a soul who finds itself in this stage to have to return to dealing with everything, to behold and see the farce of this so poorly harmonized life, to waste time in taking care of bodily needs, sleeping, and eating! Everything wearies it; it doesn't know how to flee; it sees itself captured and in chains. Then it feels more truly the misery of life and the captivity we endure because of our bodies. (L 21.6)

That which daunted me most was my lack of health, for when I have my health, everything seems easy to me. (F 31.12)

WEAKNESS

I never felt more pusillanimous or cowardly in my life. Indeed, I didn't recognize myself. (F 25.1)

When the soul begins to mortify itself, everything is painful to it. If it begins to give up comforts, it grieves; if it must give up honor, it feels torment; and if it must suffer an offensive word, the hurt becomes intolerable for it. (SS 3.12)

When [the soul] sees again the cracks and imperfections in itself, it then fears everything. (L 15.15)

Sometimes I think I am very detached; and, as a matter of fact, when put to the test, I am. At another time I will find myself so attached, and perhaps to things that the day before I would have made fun of, that I almost don't know myself. At other times I think I have great courage and that I wouldn't turn from anything of service to God; and when put to the test, I do have this courage for some things. Another day will come in which I won't find the courage in me to kill even an ant for God if in doing so I'd meet with any opposition. In like manner it seems to me that I don't care at all about things or gossip said of me; and when I'm put to the test this is at times true—indeed, I am pleased about what they say. Then there are days in which one word alone distresses me, and I would want to leave the world because it seems everything is a bother to me. (W 38.6)

To carry on a conversation with anyone is [an ordeal], for the devil gives a spirit of anger so displeasing that it seems as if I want to eat everyone up, without being able to help it; or it would seem to me an accomplishment if one could control one's temper. (L 30.13)

RESISTANCE

One day the Lord told me: "You always desire trials, and on the other hand you refuse them." (T 11)

I'm still not ready for suffering. (S 6.3)

There comes a foolishness of soul—that's what I call it—for it seems to me that I do neither good nor evil, but follow the crowd, as they say. I do so neither in pain nor in glory, nor does it give life or death, or please or weigh me down. It doesn't seem that the soul feels anything. I think it goes about like a little donkey that's grazing. (L 30.18)

I became extremely vexed about the many tears I was shedding over my faults, for neither were my resolutions nor were the hardships I suffered enough to keep me from placing myself in the occasion [of sin] and falling again. They seemed fraudulent tears to me. (L 6.4)

Very often, for some years, I was more anxious that the hour I had determined to spend in prayer be over than I was to remain there, and more anxious to listen for the striking of the clock than to attend to other good things. And I don't know what heavy penance could have come to mind that frequently I would not have gladly undertaken rather than recollect myself in the practice of prayer. . . . So unbearable was the sadness I felt on entering the oratory, that I had to muster up all my courage (and they say I have no small amount of that, and it is observed that God has given me more than women usually have, but I have made poor use of it) in order to force myself. (L 8.7)

They do not embrace the cross but drag it along, and so it hurts and wearies them and breaks them to pieces. (SS 2.26)

REVULSION

Deliver me, Lord, from this shadow of death, deliver me from so many trials, deliver me from so many sufferings, deliver me from so many changes, from so many compliments that we are forced to receive while still living, from so many, many, many things that tire and weary me, that would tire anyone reading this if I mentioned them all. (W 42.2)

Oh, how different this life would have to be for one not to desire death! How our will deviates in its inclination from that which is the will of God. He wants us to love truth; we love the lie. He wants us to desire the eternal; we, here below, lean toward what comes to an end. He wants us to desire sublime and great things; we, here below, desire base and earthly things. He would want us to desire only what is secure; we, here below, love the dubious. Everything is a mockery. (W 42.4)

The contempt that was left in me for everything earthly was great; these things all seemed to me like dung, and I see how basely we are occupied, those of us who are detained by earthly things. (L 38.3)

DRYNESS IN PRAYER

But what will they do here who see that after many days there is nothing but dryness, distaste, vapidness, and very little desire to come to draw water? . . . This gardener helps Christ carry the cross and reflects that the Lord lived with it all during His life. He doesn't desire the Lord's kingdom here below or ever abandon prayer. And so he is determined, even though this dryness may last his whole life, not to let Christ fall with the cross. The time will come when the Lord will repay him all at once. He doesn't fear that the labor is being wasted. He is serving a good Master whose eyes are upon him. (L 11.10)

It isn't always good to abandon prayer when there is great distraction and disturbance in the intellect, just as it isn't always good to torture the soul into doing what it cannot do.

There are other exterior things [that can be done] like works of charity and spiritual reading, although at times [the soul] will not even be fit for these. Let it then serve the body out of love of God—because many other times the body serves the soul—and engage in some spiritual pastimes such as holy conversations, provided they are truly so, or going to the country. (L 11.16)

It is very important that no one be distressed or afflicted over dryness or noisy and distracting thoughts. If a person wishes to gain freedom of spirit and not be always troubled, let him begin by not being frightened by the cross, and he will see how the Lord also helps him carry it, and he will gain satisfaction and profit from everything. For, clearly, if the well is dry, we cannot put water into it. (L 11.17)

DISTRACTION IN PRAYER

I was grieved because I was so distracted I couldn't concentrate. So I complained to the Lord about our miserable nature. (T 13.1)

The mind wandered here and there. My soul, it seems to me, was like a bird flying about that doesn't know where to light; and it was losing a lot of time and not making progress in virtue or improving in prayer. (IC VI.7.15)

The imagination and memory carry on such a war that the soul is left powerless. . . . They don't rest in anything but flit from one thing to another; they are like little moths at night, bothersome and annoying; so they go from one extreme to another. (L 17.6)

This intellect is so wild that it doesn't seem to be anything else than a frantic madman no one can tie down; nor am I master of it. . . . And so I say to the Lord, "When, my God, will I finally see my soul joined together in Your praise, so that all its faculties may enjoy You? Do not permit, Lord, that it be broken any longer in pieces, for it only seems that each piece goes its own way."

I often undergo this scattering of the faculties. (L 30.16)

Should [the soul] want to remedy the situation by reading, it would feel as though it didn't know how to read. Once it happened that I started to read a life of a saint to see if it would absorb me, and to console myself by what he suffered; after reading a number of lines four or five times, I understood less from them than I did at the beginning, and so I stopped. This happened to me often. (L 30.12)

Sometimes I want to die in that I cannot cure this wandering of the intellect. (W 31.8)

I began to envy those who live in deserts and to think that since they don't hear or see anything, they are free of this wandering of the mind. I heard: "You are greatly mistaken, daughter; rather, the temptations of the devil there are stronger. Be patient, for as long as you live, a wandering mind cannot be avoided." (T 39.1)

The only remedy I have found, after having tired myself out for many years, is . . . to pay no more attention to the memory than one would to a madman—leave it to go its way, for only God can stop it, and, in truth, here it remains a slave. We must suffer it with patience. (L 17.7)

Pay no attention to the intellect, for it is a grinding mill. (L 15.6)

SILENT PRAYER

The soul will lose a great deal if it isn't careful in this matter, especially if the intellect is keen. For when the soul begins to compose speeches and search for ideas, though insignificant, it will think it is doing something if they are well expressed. . . . There isn't any idea that will make God give us so great a favor. . . . [We should pray] not with the noise of words but with longing that He hear us. (L 15.7)

He will understand us as if through sign language. . . . He doesn't want us to be breaking our heads trying to speak a great deal to Him. (W 29.6)

All the harm comes from not truly understanding that He is near, but in imagining Him as far away. . . . It isn't necessary to shout to speak to Him. (W 29.5)

I'm not asking you now that you think about Him or that you draw out a lot of concepts or make long and subtle reflections with your intellect. I'm not asking you to do anything more than look at Him. . . .
    If you are joyful, look at Him as risen. Just imagining

74

how He rose from the tomb will bring you joy. The brilliance! The beauty! The majesty! How victorious! How joyful! Indeed, like one coming forth from a battle where he has gained a great kingdom! . . .

If you are experiencing trials or are sad, behold Him on the way to the garden: what great affliction He bore in His soul; for having become suffering itself, He tells us about it and complains of it. . . . He will look at you with those eyes so beautiful and compassionate, filled with tears; He will forget His sorrows so as to console you in yours, merely because you yourselves go to Him to be consoled, and you turn your head to look at Him. (W 26.3–5)

8

SHATTERING

INTERIOR SUFFERING

My heart broke. (L 9.1)

Oh, God help me, what interior and exterior trials the soul suffers before entering the seventh dwelling place. (IC VI.1.1)

Oh, were we to treat of interior sufferings, these others would seem small if the interior ones could be clearly explained; but it is impossible to explain the way in which they come to pass. (IC VI.1.7)

The pain suffered in this state . . . breaks and grinds the soul into pieces. (IC V.2.11)

DOUBT AND CONFUSION

I feared, since I saw I was so wretched, that the favors the Lord had granted me had been illusions. (L 39.20)

It then seems to the soul that it has never been mindful of God and never will be; and when it hears His Majesty spoken of, it seems to it as though it were hearing about a person far away. (IC VI.1.8)

The soul doesn't think that it has any love of God or that it ever had any, for if it has done some good, or His Majesty has granted it some favor, all this seems to have been dreamed up or fancied. (IC VI.1.11)

The intellect became so stupefied that it made me walk in the midst of a thousand doubts and suspicions. (L 30.8)

All that the Lord had commanded me, and the great deal of advice, and the prayers that for more than two years had gone on almost without cease, all was erased from my memory as though it had never been. (L 36.7)

I didn't know what I was saying. (L 9.1)

My soul was left as though in a desert, very disconsolate and fearful. I didn't know what to do with myself. (L 24.4

FEAR

Everything made me afraid. (L 30.13)

I saw danger everywhere. I was like a person in the middle of a river trying to get out; wherever she goes, she fears greater peril there; and she is almost drowning. . . . I was frightened and scared. With the serious heart trouble I had, I'm amazed that much damage wasn't done to me. . . . I didn't know what to do; I was all tears. . . . I was terribly distressed and in the greatest anguish. (L 23.12,13,15)

Oh, God help me, what a miserable life this is! There's no secure happiness, nor anything that doesn't change. A short time before, it seemed to me I wouldn't change my happiness with anyone on earth, and now the very reason for this happiness tormented me in such a way that I didn't know what to do with myself. Oh, if we would carefully observe the affairs of our life! Each one would see through experience the little of either happiness or unhappiness he ought to have on their account. (L 36.9)

MISUNDERSTANDING

There was no one in this city who understood me. (L 30.6)

Criticism of me increased. . . . I was very much disliked. They said I was insulting them. (L 33.1-2)

What caused me great anguish was something my confessor once wrote to me . . . in the midst of this multitude of persecutions, when I thought comfort would be coming from him. . . . What he said grieved me more than everything else put together. . . . This made me so extremely distressed I was thrown into complete confusion and severely afflicted. (L 33.3)

May it please the Lord to deliver us from times when we have to fear doing things that are perfectly good because

there are eyes that are fixed on all we do with such passionate hatred. (LE 227)

Those she considered her friends turn away from her,
and they are the ones who take the largest, most painful
bite at her. . . . What is worse, these things do not pass
quickly, but go on throughout the person's whole life.
(IC VI.1.3–4)

There were enough things to drive me insane, and sometimes I found myself in such straits that I didn't know
what to do other than raise my eyes to the Lord. For the
opposition of good men to a little woman, wretched,
weak, and fearful like myself, seems to be nothing when
described in so few words, yet among the very severe
trials I suffered in my life, this was one of the most severe. (L 28.18)

DISTRESS

I remained for a long time totally dissolved in tears and
feeling within myself utter distress and weariness. Oh,
how a soul suffers, God help me, by losing the freedom
it should have in being itself; and what torments it un-
dergoes! I marvel now at how I could have lived in such
great affliction. (L 9.8)

Woe is me, woe is me, Lord, how very long is this exile!
And it passes with great sufferings of longing for my
God! Lord, what can a soul placed in this prison do? O
Jesus, how long is the life of man, even though it is said
to be short! (S 15.1)

Well then, what will this poor soul do when the torment goes on for many days? If it prays, it feels as though it hasn't prayed—as far as consolation goes, I mean. For consolation is not admitted into the soul's interior, nor is what one recites to oneself, even though vocal, understood. As for mental prayer, this definitely is not the time for that, because the faculties are incapable of the practice; rather, solitude causes greater harm—and also another torment for this soul is to be with anyone or to have others speak to it. And thus however much it wills itself not to do so, it goes about with a gloomy and ill-tempered mien that is externally very noticeable. (IC VI.1.13)

Is it true that it will know how to explain its experiences? They are indescribable, for they are spiritual afflictions and sufferings that one cannot name. The best remedy (I don't mean for getting rid of them, because I don't find any, but so that they may be endured) is to engage in external works of charity and to hope in the mercy of God who never fails those who hope in Him. (IC VI.1.13)

Many are the things that war against it with an interior oppression so keen and unbearable that I don't know what to compare this experience to, if not to the oppression of those who suffer in hell, for no consolation is allowed in the midst of this tempest. . . . If a person in this state who knows how to read well takes up a book in the vernacular, he will find that he understands no more of it than if he didn't know how to read even one of the letters, for the intellect is incapable of understanding. (IC VI.1.9)

I became angry with myself in such a way that I then truly hated myself. (L 40.20)

ILLNESS

Sometimes it seemed that sharp teeth were biting into me, so much so that it was feared I had rabies. With the continuous fever and the great lack of strength (for because of nausea I wasn't able to eat anything, only drink), I was so shriveled and wasted away (because for almost a month they gave me a daily purge) that my nerves began to shrink, causing such unbearable pains that I found no rest either by day or by night—a very deep sadness. (L 5.7)

Only the Lord can know the unbearable torments I suffered within myself: my tongue, bitten to pieces; my throat unable to let even water pass down—from not having swallowed anything and from great weakness that oppressed me; everything seeming to be disjointed; the greatest confusion in my head; all shriveled and drawn together in a ball. (L 6.1)

If these pains are severe, the trial is, it seems to me, the greatest on earth—I mean the greatest exterior trial, however many the other pains. I say "if the pains are severe," because they then afflict the soul interiorly and exteriorly in such a way that it doesn't know what to do with itself. It would willingly accept at once any martyrdom rather than these sharp pains. (IC VI.1.6)

I find eating mutton so bad for me that I can take nothing but poultry. My whole trouble is weakness. . . . I am really irritated to discover I am so useless: this body of mine does me harm and keeps me from doing good. (LE 171)

EXHAUSTION

Well, my soul was now tired; and, in spite of its desire, my wretched habits would not allow it rest. (L 9.1)

I had hardly slept the whole night, nor had I been without work or worry some of the other nights; and all the days had been truly tiring. (L 36.11)

I had so much correspondence and business to attend to that day that I was writing till two in the morning, which gave me a dreadful headache. . . . I have been doing too much this winter, and it is all my fault, for I have been robbing myself of sleep at night so that I should be free in the mornings. (LE 168)

When I came here, it seemed quite impossible that, with my poor health and weak constitution, I could stand up to so much work; for business connected with these convents is going on all the time, and then, quite apart from this house, there are any number of things that would be enough to wear me out. (LE 34)

So many troubles are descending on me all at once that they sometimes make me very tired. (LE 208)

BUSY-NESS

You would be shocked if you knew about all the troubles I am having here, and all the business I have to do—it is killing me. (LE 432)

I have had so many letters during the last two days that they have driven me crazy. (LE 111)

We are on a journey and, with all the business I have to do, I hardly know where I am. (LE 437)

I assure you, the Lord does not leave me much leisure. (LE 207)

I can tell you I get very little relaxation and have many troubles. (LE 378)

WORRY

These murders being committed on the roads are a nightmare to me. (LE 243)

It worries me that things should cost so much, and there are a great many expenses that keep arising. (LE 101)

I didn't know what to do or how to pay some workmen. (L 33.12)

Oh, Jesus, how dreadful it is to be so far away when all these things are going on! I assure you it is a heavy cross for me. (LE 98)

I am shocked and grieved about those two souls: God help them. It seems just as though all the furies of hell have joined together at Seville, and are deceiving and blinding people both within the community and without. . . . That wretched vicaress was always making up such dreadful calumnies: for a long time I have been afraid this would happen. Oh, Jesus, what a weight on my mind it has been! None of the trials we have gone through has been anything by comparison with this. (LE 271)

SEPARATION AND DEATH

Don't think the matter lies in my being so conformed to the will of God that if my father or brother dies I don't feel it, or that if there are trials or sicknesses I suffer them happily. (IC V.3.7)

I remember, clearly and truly, that when I left my father's house I felt that separation so keenly that the feeling will not be greater, I think, when I die. For it seemed that every bone in my body was being sundered. Since there was no love of God to take away my love for my father and relatives, everything so constrained me that if the Lord hadn't helped me, my reflections would not have been enough for me to continue on. (L 4.1)

I felt it very much when he went away, although I didn't try to prevent him. . . . I was very troubled about his leaving. (L 33.5)

And to leave my daughters and Sisters, when going from one place to another, was not the smallest cross, I tell you, since I love them so much—especially when I thought I was not going to return to see them again. (F 27.18)

All day yesterday I felt very lonely, for except when I received Communion, I benefited little from the fact that it was Easter Sunday. . . . Since [you] went away so quickly yesterday (and I realize that your many occupations do not allow you time to be consoling me, even when necessary) . . . I remained afflicted and sad. (T 12.1,4)

At this time my father was seized with an illness that lasted for some days and from which he died. . . . In losing him I was losing every good and joy. . . . It seemed my soul was being wrenched from me, for I loved him dearly. (L 7.14)

LONELINESS

I am suffering just now from the isolation we feel so much at Toledo. Oh, what frosts we get here! It is almost as bad as at Ávila; and yet I am well, though I long to see a letter from one of you—it seems such a time since I had one last. The couriers, too, are as slow in coming to us as in going to you. But the fact is, things always seem to go slowly when you are longing for them. (LE 159)

I never imagined you would forget me. (LE 20)

I have no one to discuss things with and get relief in that way, but I always have to think everything out for myself. (LE 34)

I sometimes get such longings to see you that I seem able to think of nothing else: that is the truth. (LE 107)

I feel very lonely in this place and have no one to turn to for comfort. God help me—the farther I journey in this life, the less comfort I find. (LE 378)

It is wrong of you to let such a long time pass without writing to me, for you know how I like your letters. God be with you. I am feeling very keenly disappointed at being unable to see you, as I had been hoping all the time to do. (LE 62)

I should not be human if I did not feel returning [to Ávila] very keenly, with my brother and my friends gone, and the worst thing is what the people are like who remain. (LE 375)

ANXIETY OVER OTHERS

Suppose we were to see a Christian with his hands fastened behind his back by a strong chain, bound to a post, and dying of hunger, not because of lack of food, for there are very choice dishes beside him, but because he cannot take hold of the food and eat, and even has great loathing for it; and suppose he sees he is about to breathe his last and die, not just an earthly death but an eternal one. Wouldn't it be a terrible cruelty to stand looking at him and not feed him? Well, then, what if through your prayer the chain could be loosened? (IC VII.1.4)

I am now in Segovia, and feel extremely worried, as I shall continue to do till I know how you are. (LE 324)

If only I could be with you now that you are having such an anxious time. How right you are to tell your troubles to one who has a fellow-feeling with your distress. (LE 145)

Though I have been suffering some here myself, I have been more oppressed by your [suffering]. But I have been in the grip of depression and am not yet free from it. (LE 418)

All yesterday, Wednesday, my heart was aching, for I could not bear to see you worrying so—and quite justifiably—scenting danger in everything. . . . The Lord has looked for a good way of making me suffer by willing that the blows should fall in a place where they will hurt me more than if they fell on me. (LE 242)

I am astounded they are telling you to get up in weather like this. For pity's sake, do not do so: it is enough to kill you. (LE 152)

For the love of God, do not preach so many sermons this Lent or eat such bad fish; you don't realize it, but it does you much harm, and then you get those temptations. (LE 349)

Whatever anyone says, be sure not to take sarsaparilla water, and for the love of God, don't be careless and let the fever go on without taking medicine for it. (LE 118)

I keep thinking of what they did to Fray John of the Cross. I don't know how God can allow such things. Even [you] do not know the full story. For all these nine months he has been in a little cell, which would hardly hold him, small though he is; and all that time, though he had been at death's door, he never once changed his tunic. Three days before he escaped, the Subprior gave him a shirt of his own and some hard disciplines. He saw no one.

I envy him very keenly. Our Lord indeed gave him abundant stores of strength for such a martyrdom. It is well that this should be known, so that people may be more on their guard against these folk. God forgive them.

Information should be laid before the Nuncio to show him what those people did with this saint of a Fray John, who had committed no fault whatever. It is a piteous story. (LE 246)

PRAYER IN ANGUISH

My God, how sad is
Life without You!
Longing to see You,
Death I desire.

This earth's journey,
How long it is;
A painful dwelling,
An exile drear.
Oh, Master adored,
Take me away!
Longing to see You,
Death I desire . . .

Afflicted, my soul
Sighs and faints.
Ah, who can stay apart
From her Beloved?
Oh! End now,
This my suffering.
Longing to see You,
Death I desire . . .

When at last
You enter my heart,
My God, then at once
I fear your leaving.
The pain that touches me
Makes me say,
Longing to see You,
Death I desire . . .

Ah! may my tears gain
Your listening to me:
Longing to see You,
Death I desire. (P 7)

9

GLORY

HIGHEST PERFECTION

Even from here below you can begin to enjoy glory!
(W 40.9)

The highest perfection obviously does not consist in interior delights or in great raptures or in visions or in the spirit of prophecy, but in having our will so much in conformity with God's will that there is nothing we know He wills that we do not want with all our desire, and in accepting the bitter as happily as we do the delightful when we know that His Majesty desires it. This seems most difficult (not the doing of it, but this being content with what completely contradicts our nature); and indeed it truly is difficult. But love has this strength if it is perfect, for we forget about pleasing ourselves in order to please the one we love. And truly this is so, for even though the trials may be very great, they become sweet when we know we are pleasing to God. And this is the way by which those who have reached this stage love persecutions, dishonor, and offenses. (F 5.10)

Blame does not intimidate the soul but strengthens it. Experience has already taught it the wonderful gain that comes through this path. . . . And since it clearly experiences the benefits of persecution, it acquires a special and very tender love for its persecutors. It seems to it that they are greater friends and more advantageous than those who speak well of it. (IC VI.1.5)

Oh, how everything that is suffered with love is healed again! (W 16.7)

If it were necessary to be always annihilated for the greater honor of God, love would do so very eagerly. (IC VI.9.18)

HOLY INDIFFERENCE

A soul surrendered into God's hands doesn't care whether [people] say good or evil about it. (L 31.16)

The soul God brings to Himself in so sublime a contemplation is not touched by these wrongs, nor does it care at all whether it is esteemed or not. I didn't say this well, "nor does it care at all," for it is much more afflicted by honor than by dishonor and by a lot of ease and rest than by trials. . . . Just as others prize gold and jewels, they prize trials and desire them; they know that these latter are what make them rich. . . . Self-esteem is far removed from these persons. (W 36.8–10)

Since I was so sickly, I have always been tied down without being worth anything until I determined to pay no attention to the body or to my health. Now what I do doesn't amount to much; but since God desired that I understand this trick of the devil, who put the thought in my head that I would lose my health, I said: What difference does it make if I die; or at the thought of rest, I answered: I no longer need rest but the cross; and so with other thoughts. I have seen clearly on very many occasions, even though I am in fact very sickly, that it was a temptation from the devil or from my own laziness—for afterward when I wasn't so cared for and pampered, I had much better health. (L 13.7)

Bodily strength is not necessary but only love and a habit. (L 7.12)

In the cross, my glory. (P 26)

FREEDOM

I have never again been able to tie myself to any friendship or to find consolation in or bear particular love for any other person than those I understand love Him and strive to serve Him; nor is it in my power to do so, nor does it matter whether they are friends or relatives. (L 24.6)

What do kings and lords matter to me if I don't want their riches, or don't care to please them, if in order to do so I would have to displease God in even the smallest thing? (W 2.5)

How rich he will find that he is, he who has left all riches for Christ! How honored will he be, he who has not sought honor from Him but has enjoyed seeing himself humbled! How wise will he be, he who rejoiced to be considered mad because that is what they called Wisdom Himself! (L 27.14)

> Give me death, give me life,
> Health or sickness,
> Honor or shame,
> War or swelling peace,
> Weakness or full strength,
> Yes to these, I say. (P 2)

PEACE

In one way or another, there must be a cross while we live. And with respect to anyone who says that after he arrived here he always enjoyed rest and delight, I would say that he never arrived. . . .

I don't mean to say that those who arrive here do not have peace; they do have it, and it is very deep. For the trials themselves are so valuable and have such good roots that although very severe, they give rise to peace and happiness. (IC V.2.8–10)

That there are trials and sufferings and that at the same time the soul is in peace is a difficult thing to explain. (IC VII.2.10)

The cross is not wanting, but it doesn't disquiet or make them lose peace. For the storms, like a wave, pass quickly. And the fair weather returns, because the presence of the Lord they experience makes them soon forget everything. (IC VII.3.15)

This soul is no longer in part subject to the miseries of the world as it used to be. For although it suffers more, this is only on the surface. The soul is like a lord in his castle, and so it doesn't lose its peace, although this security doesn't remove a great fear of offending God and of not getting rid of all that would be a hindrance to serving Him. The soul rather proceeds more cautiously, but it goes about so forgetful of self that it thinks it has partly lost its being. In this state everything is directed to the honor of God, to the greater fulfillment of His will, and to His glory. (T 65.1)

SURRENDER

There is no other reason for living than to suffer trials, and this is what I most willingly beg of God. Sometimes I say earnestly to Him: "Lord, either to die or to suffer; I don't ask anything else for myself." I am consoled to hear the clock strike, for at the passing away of that hour of life it seems to me that I am drawing a little closer to the vision of God. (L 40.20)

It is advisable . . . to abandon oneself completely into the hands of God: if He wants to bring the soul to heaven, it goes; if to hell, it feels no grief, since it goes with God; if its life comes to an end, this it desires; if it lives a thousand years, this too it desires. Let His Majesty treat it as His own—the soul no longer belongs to itself. It is given over entirely to the Lord—it completely overlooks itself. (L 17.2)

Your will, Lord, be done in me in every way and manner that You, my Lord, want. If You want it to be done with trials, strengthen me and let them come; if with persecutions, illnesses, dishonors, and a lack of life's necessities, here I am; I will not turn away, my Father, nor is it right that I turn my back on You. (W 32.10)

From here on the soul desires nothing for itself; it wants its actions to be in complete conformity with His glory and His will. (L 20.22)

Here is my life, here is my honor and my will. I have given all to You, I am Yours. Make use of me according to Your will. (L 21.5)

HUMILITY

How necessary [self-knowledge] is—see that you understand me—even for those whom the Lord has brought into the very dwelling place where He abides. For never, however exalted the soul may be, is anything else fitting for it; nor could it be even were the soul to so desire. For humility, like the bee making honey in the beehive, is always at work. Without it, everything goes wrong. (IC I.2.8)

This path of self-knowledge must never be abandoned, nor is there on this journey a soul so much a giant that it has no need to return often to the stage of an infant and suckling. And this should never be forgotten. Perhaps I shall speak of it more often because it is very important. There is no stage of prayer so sublime that it isn't necessary to return often to the beginning. Along this path of prayer, self-knowledge and the thought of one's sins is the bread with which all palates must be fed no matter how delicate they may be; they cannot be sustained without this bread. (L 13.15)

VICTORY

In this prayer, wings sprout, enabling one to fly with ease; the fledgling has shed its down; in this prayer Christ's banner is now completely raised. It seems just as though the custodian of this fortress climbs, or is taken up, to the highest tower to raise the banner for God. He looks at those below as one who is out of danger. He no longer fears dangers but rather desires them as someone who in a certain manner receives assurance there of victory. In [this prayer], the soul sees very clearly how little everything here below should be esteemed and the trifle that it is. Whoever stands upon a height sees many things. The soul no longer wants to desire, nor would it want to have free will—and this is what I beg the Lord. [The soul] gives Him the keys of its will. (L 20.22)

We are His slaves, our wills being sold, out of love for Him, through the virtue of obedience. (F 5.17)

Refraining from doing one's own will is more fitting than the experience of consolation. (F 6.16)

Those who in fact risk all for God will find that they have both lost all and gained all. (L 16.7)

May what I have said help . . . encourage us to walk with fortitude along a road that has such rugged mountain passes, as does that of this life, but not intimidate us from walking through them. For, in the final analysis, by proceeding with humility, through the mercy of God we will reach that city of Jerusalem, where all that has been suffered will be little or nothing in comparison with what is enjoyed. (F 4.4)

HAPPY DEATH

It will be a great thing at the hour of death to see that we are going to be judged by the One whom we have loved above all things. . . . It will not be like going to a foreign country but like going to our own, because it is the country of One whom we love so much and who loves us. (W 40.8)

Little fear of death, which I always feared greatly, remained. Now death seems to me to be the easiest thing for anyone who serves God, for in a moment the soul finds it is freed from this prison and brought to rest. (L 38.5)

O death, death, I don't know who fears you, since life lies in you! (S 6.2)

CONTEMPLATIVE PRAYER

Prayer is not experienced as work but as glory. (L 18.1)

This water from heaven often comes when the gardener is least expecting it. True, in the beginning it almost always occurs after a long period of mental prayer. The Lord comes to take this tiny bird from one degree to another and to place it in the nest so that it may have repose. Since He has seen it fly about for a long time, striving with the intellect and the will and all its strength to see God and please Him, He desires to reward it even in this life. And what a tremendous reward; one moment is enough to repay all the trials that can be suffered in this life! (L 18.9)

The soul understands that without the noise of words, this divine Master is teaching it by suspending its faculties, for if they were to be at work, they would do harm rather than bring benefit. They are enjoying without understanding how they are enjoying. The soul is being enkindled in love, and it doesn't understand how it loves. It knows that it enjoys what it loves, but it doesn't know how. It clearly understands that this joy is not a joy the intellect obtains merely through desire. The will is enkindled without understanding how. But as soon as it can understand something, it sees that this good cannot be merited or gained through all the trials one can suffer on earth. This good is a gift from the Lord of earth and heaven, who, in sum, gives according to who He is. What I have described, daughters, is perfect contemplation. (W 25.2)

If a person is reflecting upon some scriptural event, it becomes as lost to the memory as it would be if there had never been any thought of it. If the person reads, there is no remembrance of what he read; nor is there any remembrance if he prays vocally. Thus this bothersome little moth, which is the memory, gets its wings burnt here; it can no longer move. The will is fully occupied in loving, but it doesn't understand how it loves. The intellect, if it understands, doesn't understand how it understands; at least it can't comprehend anything of what it understands. It doesn't seem to me that it understands, because, as I say, it doesn't understand—I really can't understand this! (L 18.14)

IMPASSIONED CONCERN

How forgetful this soul, in which the Lord dwells in so particular a way, should be of its own rest, how little it should care for its honor, and how far it should be from wanting esteem in anything! For if it is with Him very much, as is right, it should think little about itself. All its concern is taken up with how to please Him more and how or where it will show Him the love it bears Him. This is the reason for prayer, my daughters, the purpose of this spiritual marriage: the birth always of good works, good works. (IC VII.4.6)

Do you know what it means to be truly spiritual? It means becoming the slaves of God. Marked with His brand, which is that of the cross, spiritual persons, because now they have given Him their liberty, can be sold by Him as slaves of everyone, as He was. (IC VII.4.8)

The glory [of truly spiritual people] lies in being able some way to help the Crucified, especially when they see He is so offended and that few there are who, detached

from everything else, really look after His honor.
(IC VII.3.6)

All my longing was and still is that since He has so many
enemies and so few friends, that these friends be good
ones. . . .
    What is the matter with Christians nowadays? Must
it always be those who owe You the most who afflict
You? Those for whom You performed the greatest
works, those You have chosen for Your friends?
(W 1.2,3)

CONTEMPLATION IN ACTION

Let us desire and be occupied in prayer, not for the sake
of our enjoyment, but so as to have this strength to
serve. (IC VII.4.12)

Enjoyment in prayer is not so habitual that there is not
time for everything. (IC VI.7.13)

In this prayer [the soul] can also be Martha, in such a
way that it is as though engaged in both the active and
contemplative life together. It tends to works of charity
and to business affairs that have to do with its state in
life. . . . And it understands clearly that the best part of
the soul is somewhere else. It's as though we were speaking to someone at our side and from the other side another person were speaking to us. . . . This prayer is
something that is felt very clearly, and it gives deep satisfaction and happiness when it is experienced. It is an
excellent preparation so that the soul may reach a pro-

found quiet when it has time for solitude, or leisure from business matters. (L 17.4)

You need not be desiring to benefit the whole world but must concentrate on those who are in your company, and thus your deed will be greater since you are more obliged toward them. (IC VII.4.14)

> If You want me to rest,
> I desire it for love;
> If to labor,
> I will die working:
> Sweet Love say
> Where, how, and when. (P 2)

Love turns work into rest. (S 5.2)

FRUITION

This prayer and union leaves the greatest tenderness in the soul in such a way that it would want to be consumed not from pain but from joyous tears. . . . It sometimes happened to me in this kind of prayer that I was so taken out of myself that I didn't know whether I was dreaming or whether the glory I was experiencing was indeed occurring. (L 19.1)

The soul becomes so courageous that if at that moment it were cut in pieces for God, it would be greatly consoled. Such prayer is the source of heroic promises, of resolutions, and of ardent desires. . . . [The soul's] humility is deeper because it sees plainly that through no diligence of its own did it receive that very generous and magnificent gift, and that it played no role in obtaining or experiencing it. Since there is no hidden cobweb in a room where much sun enters, the soul sees clearly that it is most unworthy; it sees misery. Vainglory goes off so far that it doesn't seem possible for the soul to have any. Since there is hardly even any consent there, it now with its own eyes sees it is capable of little or nothing. It seems, though it didn't desire this, that the door of all the senses was closed to it that it might be better able to enjoy the Lord. It remains alone with Him. What has it to do but love Him? It neither sees nor hears save by much effort. There is not much to thank the soul for. Afterward, with striking truth, its past life and the great mercy of God are shown to it. The intellect doesn't have to go hunting for this knowledge because it beholds there, all cooked and prepared, what it must eat and understand. It perceives that it merits hell and that yet it is chastised with glory. (L 19.2)

For at an unexpected time, with one word alone or a chance happening, He so quickly calms the storm that it seems there had not been even as much as a cloud in that soul, and it remains filled with sunlight and much more consolation. And like one who has escaped from a dangerous battle and been victorious, it comes out praising our Lord; for it was He who fought for the victory. (IC VI.1.10)

> Let nothing disturb you,
> Nothing dismay you.
> All things are passing,
> God never changes.

Patient endurance
Obtains all things.
Whom God possesses
In nothing is wanting.
God alone suffices. (Bookmark Prayer)

What God communicates here to the soul in an instant is a secret so great and a favor so sublime—and the delight the soul experiences is so extreme—that I don't know what to compare it to. I can only say that the Lord wishes to reveal for that moment, in a more sublime manner than through any spiritual vision or taste, the glory of heaven. (IC VII.2.3)

10

DIVINE INTIMACY

PAY NOW

May You be blessed forever and ever, my God, for within a moment You undo a soul and remake it. (F 22.7)

Oh, oh, how well He pays! And He pays without measure! (W 37.3)

The Lord did not let His poor servant suffer long, for never did He fail to succor me in my tribulations. (L 36.9)

I would not exchange those trials for all the world's treasures. (SS 6.1–2)

If His Majesty repays so fully that even in this life the reward and gain possessed by those who serve Him is clearly seen, what will this reward be in the next life! (L 21.12)

It is a great thing to have experienced the friendship and favor He shows toward those who journey on this road and how He takes care of almost all the expenses. (W 23.5)

You already know there is the hundredfold even in this life and that the Lord says, "Ask, and you will receive." If you don't believe His Majesty in the sections of His Gospel that ensure this gain, it will be of little benefit, Sisters, for me to break my head in trying to tell you about it. (W 23.6)

The journey of prayer . . . brings with it the following good: more is given than is asked for, beyond what we could desire. This is absolutely true; I know. (W 23.6)

He promised me there wasn't anything I might ask Him that He wouldn't do; that He already knew I wouldn't ask for anything other than what was in conformity with His glory; . . . there wasn't anything I asked for that He didn't grant, and in a better way than I knew how to ask for. (L 39.1)

I have seen clearly that God does not leave one, even in this life, without a large reward; because it is certainly true that one of those hours in which the Lord afterward bestowed on me a taste of Himself repaid, it seems to me, all the anguish I suffered in persevering for a long time in prayer. (L 11.11)

This suffering was well repaid, for almost always the favors afterward came in great abundance. I only think that the soul comes out of the crucible like gold, more refined and purified, so as to see the Lord within itself. (L 30.14)

DIVINE INTIMACY

Prayer in my opinion is nothing else than an intimate sharing between friends; it means taking time frequently to be alone with Him who we know loves us. (L 8.5)

He begins to commune with the soul in so intimate a friendship that He not only gives it back its own will, but gives it His. For in so great a friendship the Lord takes joy in putting the soul in command. (W 32.12)

Oh, my Lord, my Mercy, and my Good! And what greater good could I want in this life than to be so close to You, that there be no division between You and me? With this companionship, what can be difficult? What can one not undertake for You, being so closely joined? (SS 4.9)

God and the soul understand each other. . . . It's like the experience of two persons here on earth who love each other deeply and understand each other well; even without signs, just by a glance, it seems, they understand each other. . . . These two lovers gaze directly at each other, as the Bridegroom says to the Bride in the *Song of Songs*. (L 27.10)

PRAYER AS LOVING

I have run into some for whom it seems the whole business lies in thinking. . . . I do not deny that it is a favor from the Lord if someone is able to be always meditating on His works, and it is good that one strive to do so.

However, it must be understood that not all imaginations are by their nature capable of this meditating, but all souls are capable of loving. . . . The soul is not the mind, nor is the will directed by thinking, for this would be very unfortunate. Hence, the soul's progress does not lie in thinking much but in loving much. (F 5.2)

O Jesus and my Lord! How valuable is Your love to us here! It holds our love so bound that it doesn't allow it the freedom during that time to love anything else but You. (L 14.2)

Since *my Beloved is for me and I for my Beloved,* who will be able to separate and extinguish two fires so enkindled? It would amount to laboring in vain, for the two fires have become one. (T 16.4)

With contemplatives there is always much love, or they wouldn't be contemplatives; and so their love is clearly recognized and in many ways. It is a great fire; it cannot but shine brightly. (W 40.4)

SPIRITUAL MARRIAGE

God espouses souls spiritually. . . . Even though the comparison may be a coarse one, I cannot find another that would better explain what I mean than the sacrament of marriage. This spiritual espousal is different in kind from marriage, for in these matters that we are dealing with there is never anything that is not spiritual. Corporeal things are far distant from them, and the spiritual joys the Lord gives, when compared with the delights married people must experience, are a thousand leagues distant. (IC V.4.3)

He has desired to be so joined with the creature that, just as those who are married cannot be separated, He doesn't want to be separated from the soul. (IC VII.2.3)

In the spiritual marriage, the union is like what we have when rain falls from the sky into a river or fount; all is water, for the rain that fell from heaven cannot be divided or separated from the water of the river. Or it is like what we have when a little stream enters the sea; there is no means of separating the two. Or, like the bright light entering a room through two different windows; although the streams of light are separate when entering the room, they become one. (IC VII.2.4)

Oh, what a splendid wedding Jesus arranged! (P 30)

BRIDAL MYSTICISM

O my Jesus, who could explain the benefit that lies in throwing ourselves into the arms of this Lord of ours and making an agreement with His Majesty that I look at my Beloved, and my Beloved at me? (SS 4.8)

My Lord, I do not ask You for anything else in life but that You kiss me with the kiss of Your mouth, and that You do so in such a way that although I may want to withdraw from this friendship and union, my will may always, Lord of my life, be subject to Your will and not depart from it; that there will be nothing to impede me from being able to say: "My God and my Glory, indeed

Your breasts are better and more delightful than wine."
(SS 3.15)

> Oh, what good unequaled!
> Oh, marriage most sacred!
> That the King of Majesty
> Should be Betrothed. (P 28)

Your Spouse never takes His eyes off you. . . . He is not
waiting for anything else, as He says to the bride, than
that we look at Him. In the measure you desire Him,
you will find Him. (W 26.3)

O true King, and how right the bride was in giving You
this name! For a moment You can give riches and place
them in a soul that they may be enjoyed forever. How
well ordered love is in this soul! (SS 6.11)

HOLY INTOXICATION

He brings her into the wine cellar so that she may come
out more abundantly enriched. It doesn't seem the King
wants to keep anything from her. He wants her to drink
in conformity with her desire and become wholly inebri-
ated, drinking of all the wines in God's storehouse. Let
the soul rejoice in these joys. Let it admire God's grandeurs. Let it not fear to lose its life from drinking so
much beyond what its natural weakness can endure. Let
it die in this paradise of delights. Blessed be such a death
that so makes one live! (SS 6.3)

The blessing is the greatest that can be tasted in this life,
even if all the delights and pleasures of the world were

joined together. . . . Let worldly people worry about their lordships, riches, delights, honors, and food, for even if a person were able to enjoy all these things without the accompanying trials—which is impossible—he would not attain in a thousand years the happiness that in one moment is enjoyed by a soul brought here by the Lord. (SS 4.7)

I saw close to me toward my left side an angel in bodily form. . . . The angel was not large but small; he was very beautiful, and his face was so aflame that he seemed to be one of those very sublime angels that appear to be all afire. They must belong to those they call the cherubim. . . . I saw in his hands a large golden dart, and at the end of the iron tip there appeared to be a little fire. It seemed to me this angel plunged the dart several times into my heart and that it reached deep within me. When he drew it out, I thought he was carrying off with him the deepest part of me; and he left me all on fire with great love of God. The pain was so great that it made me moan, and the sweetness this greatest pain caused me was so superabundant that there is no desire capable of taking it away; nor is the soul content with less than God. The pain is not bodily but spiritual, although the body doesn't fail to share in some of it, and even a great deal. The loving exchange that takes place between the soul and God is so sweet that I beg Him in His goodness to give a taste of this love to anyone who thinks I am lying. (L 29.13)

O true Lover, with how much compassion, with how much gentleness, with how much delight, with how much favor, and with what extraordinary signs of love You cure these wounds, which with the same darts of this same love You have caused! O my God and my rest from all pains, how entranced I am! (T 16.2)

ECSTASY

O my God and my infinite Wisdom, measureless and boundless and beyond all the human and the angelic intellects! O love that loves me more than I can love myself or understand! (S 17.1)

My King, I beseech You, that all to whom I speak become mad from Your love, or do not permit that I speak to anyone! (L 16.4)

[The soul] doesn't know whether to speak or to be silent, whether to laugh or to weep. This prayer is a glorious foolishness, a heavenly madness where the true wisdom is learned; and it is for the soul a most delightful way of enjoying. (L 16.1)

I would desire to see no other persons than those who are sick with this sickness I now have. . . . [May we] all be mad for love of Him who for love of us was called mad. (L 16.6)

Sometimes love becomes so foolish I don't make sense. (L 37.9)

Sometimes I find it a remedy to speak in absurdities. (L 18.3)

J O Y   A N D   P R A I S E

The soul would desire to have a thousand lives so as to employ them all for God, and that everything here on earth would be a tongue to help it praise Him. (IC VI.4.15)

One utters many words here in praise of God without thinking them up. . . . The soul would desire to cry out praises, and it is beside itself—a delightful disquiet. . . . It cannot bear so much joy. . . . This joy must have been what was felt in the admirable spirit of the royal prophet David when he played on the harp and sang the praises of God. I'm very devoted to this glorious king. (L 16.3)

Oh, help me, God! What is the soul like when it is in this state? It would want to be all tongues so as to praise the Lord. It speaks folly in a thousand holy ways, ever trying to find means of pleasing the One who thus possesses it. I know a person who, though not a poet, suddenly composed some deeply felt verses well expressing her pain. . . . She desired all her body and soul to break in pieces to demonstrate the joy she felt in this pain. . . . Well, it doesn't seem to me that I have exaggerated. Nothing can compare with the delight the Lord desires a soul to enjoy in this exile. (L 16.4)

[The soul] consumes itself in the praises of God—and I would want to be consumed now. May You be blessed, my Lord, that from such filthy mud as I, You make water so clear that it can be served at Your table! May

You be praised, O Joy of the angels, for having desired to raise up a worm so vile! (L 19.2)

What I'm saying seems like gibberish, but certainly the experience takes place in this way, for the joy is so excessive the soul wouldn't want to enjoy it alone but wants to tell everyone about it so that they might help this soul praise our Lord. All its activity is directed to this praise. Oh, how many festivals and demonstrations the soul would organize, if it could, that all might know its joy! (IC VI.6.10)

The joy is so great that it sometimes seems the soul is at the very point of going forth from the body. And what a happy death that would be! (L 17.1)

WOUNDS OF LOVE

Two experiences, it seems to me, which lie on this spiritual path, put a person in danger of death: the one is this pain, for it truly is a danger, and no small one; the other is overwhelming joy and delight, which reaches so extraordinary a peak that indeed the soul, I think, swoons to the point that it is hardly kept from leaving the body—indeed its happiness could not be considered small. (IC VI.11.11)

It seems as though an arrow is thrust into the heart, or into the soul itself. Thus the wound causes a severe pain that makes the soul moan; yet the pain is so delightful, the soul would never want it to go away. (T 59.17)

His action is as quick as a falling comet. And as clearly as it hears a thunderclap, even though no sound is heard, the soul understands that it was called by God. So well does it understand that sometimes, especially in the beginning, it is made to tremble and even complain without there being anything that causes it pain. It feels that it is wounded in the most exquisite way, but it doesn't learn how or by whom it was wounded. It knows clearly that the wound is something precious, and it would never want to be cured. It complains to its Spouse with words of love, even outwardly, without being able to do otherwise. It knows that He is present, but He doesn't want to reveal the manner in which He allows Himself to be enjoyed. And the pain is great, although delightful and sweet. And even if the soul does not want this wound, the wound cannot be avoided. But the soul, in fact, would never want to be deprived of this pain. (IC VI.2.2)

A pain this great is sufficient to put an end to life, but I don't merit death. All my longing then is to die; nor do I think about purgatory or of the great sins I've committed by which I've merited hell. I am oblivious of everything in that anxious longing to see God; that desert and solitude seem to the soul better than all the companionship of the world. If anything could give the soul consolation, it would be to speak to someone who had suffered this torment. (L 20.13)

I was dying with desire to see God, and I didn't know where to seek this life except in death. (L 29.8)

> I live without living in myself,
> And in such a way I hope,
> I die because I do not die. (P 1)

Holy bride, how is it that this sweetness slays you!
(SS 7.1)

JOY IN SUFFERING

What a tremendous good it is to suffer trials and persecutions for Him. For the increase of the love of God I
saw in my soul and many other things reached such a
point that I was amazed; and this makes me unable to
stop desiring trials. (L 33.4)

> *If suffering for love's sake*
> *Can give such wondrous delight,*
> *What joy will gazing on You be?*
> Love, when it has grown,
> Save in laboring cannot live,
> Nor the hearty without fighting
> Because of love for his Beloved. (P 21)

Give me trials, Lord; give me persecutions. And truly
this soul desires them and indeed passes through them
well. For since it no longer looks to its own satisfaction
but to what pleases God, its pleasure is in some way
imitating the laborious life that Christ lived. (SS 7.8)

I would always choose the path of suffering, if only to
imitate our Lord Jesus Christ if there were no other gain;
especially, since there are always so many other benefits.
(IC VI.1.7)

On another day the Lord told me this. . . . "My Father
gives greater trials to anyone whom He loves more; and
love responds to these. How can I show you greater love

than by desiring for you what I have desired for Myself?
. . . Suffering is the way of truth. By this means you will
help me weep over the loss of those who 'follow the way
of the world.' " (T 32.1)

Are you so in need, my Lord and my Love, that You
would want to receive such poor company as mine? For
I see by Your expression that You have been consoled
by me. Well, then, how is it, Lord, that the angels leave
You and that even Your Father doesn't console you? I
desire to suffer, Lord, all the trials that come to me and
esteem them as a great good enabling me to imitate You
in something. Let us walk together, Lord. Wherever You
go, I will go; whatever You suffer, I will suffer. (W 26.6)

THE CROSS

Take up that cross. . . . In stumbling, in falling with your
Spouse, do not withdraw from the cross or abandon it.
Consider carefully the fatigue with which He walks and
how much greater His trials are than those trials you
suffer, however great you may want to paint them and
no matter how much you grieve over them. You will
come out consoled because you will see that they are
something to be laughed at when compared to those of
the Lord. (W 26.7)

He wants to lead you as though you were strong, giving
you the cross here below, something that His Majesty
always had. What better friendship than that He desire
for you what He desired for Himself? (W 17.7)

O Cross, my life's delightful rest,
My welcome be.
Beneath your protecting banner,
Even the weakest are made strong! (P 18)

If the cross is loved, it is easy to bear; this is certain.
(SS 2.26)

> Within the cross is life
> And consolation.
> It alone is the road
> Leading to heaven. (P 19)